A History of Food

From Manna to Microwave

Margaret Leeming

BBC BOOKS

Published by BBC Books,
a division of BBC Enterprises Limited,
Woodlands, 80 Wood Lane, London W12 0TT
First published 1991
© Margaret Leeming 1991

ISBN 0 563 36126 3

Set in $11\frac{1}{2}/13\frac{1}{2}$ pt Garamond Roman by Butler & Tanner Ltd, Frome
Printed and bound in Great Britain by Butler & Tanner Ltd, Frome
Jacket printed by Belmont Press Ltd, Northampton

Please renew/return this item by the last date shown.

So that your telephone call is charged at local rate,
please call the numbers as set out below:

	From Area codes 01923 or 0208:	From the rest of Herts:
Renewals:	01923 471373	01438 737373
Enquiries:	01923 471333	01438 737333
Minicom:	01923 471599	01438 737599

L32b

CONTENTS

CONTENTS

ACKNOWLEDGEMENTS

Throughout the writing of this book I have received a great deal of help and kindness from many people. In particular I would like to thank Gordon Dickinson and Christine Leigh who very generously allowed me to use their personal notes on urban midday meals and modern retailing. I would like to thank David Preston who introduced me to the Mexican style of cooking turkey with chocolate, and Trudi Urmson who talked to me about her childhood in Austria, and also helped test some of the recipes. I am also extremely grateful to Julery bin Osman who so promptly and fully answered my questions concerning Muslim food. My thanks to my daughters, Alice and Anna, who each made constructive suggestions concerning some of the recipes. Above all I would like to thank my husband for his willingness to taste and give advice on all the trial recipes – not all of which were judged suitable for inclusion in this book – and for his unfailing encouragement and support throughout this work.

INTRODUCTION

Why do we eat what we eat? Our diet today is shaped mostly by fashion, by advertising, commercial pressures and the contents of the supermarket shelves; yet most of what we eat today has a history of its own. Soft white breads, a delicacy only enjoyed by the rich in medieval times, are out of fashion today, again replaced by coarser brown breads. Potatoes, first brought to England under Elizabeth I and a national staple by the time of Queen Victoria, were not linked with fish as 'fish and chips' until the 1870s. Meanwhile, the roast beef of old England has shrunk to a minute steak in recent years. In the past religion, the environment and tradition all helped shape our diet. The discovery of new lands, colonisation and the migration of peoples all introduced new foods, which over the years were absorbed into indigenous food patterns; so that tea became as British as beer. Generally speaking we give little thought to what lies behind the dishes and foods we accept as normal at our tables, but their real history is complex and fascinating.

Domestic traditions are extremely strong, and simple recipes have often survived for centuries. Kedgeree, that standby of Victorian breakfasts, started life in India before the time of Christ as a temple offering of rice and mung beans just as it still is in India today. Dried pea soup with bacon first appears in a fifteenth-century English recipe book and was probably well-established then. It is so tenacious that 600 years later it reappears in the cookery columns of a national newspaper. The brie cheeses we buy in British supermarkets are the direct descendants of those whose arrival in Paris was marked by the cries of fourteenth-century cheese sellers.

Foods travel with merchants and with migrants. The remains of two seventh-century *wuntun*, folded as they are today in Chinese restaurants around the world, have been found by archaeologists on the Silk Road to central Asia, perhaps carried there by some Chinese merchant homesick for familiar delicacies. Chocolate, the Aztec drink of the gods, when it arrived in England started a fashion for chocolate houses, one of which has survived as a London club. Samosas, now a popular snack in Britain introduced by the immigrant Indian community, were noticed in the seventeenth century by an English visitor to Persia, but they were also described in detail in a poem from Baghdad 400 years earlier. They had apparently journeyed to northern India with Persian invaders during the intervening centuries, for in the fourteenth century an Arab traveller to northern India described the samosas he ate there.

The study of food history tells us about the past in a surprisingly detailed and intimate way and also enlarges our understanding of our community and the world we live in. It is one of the few kinds of history which can involve practical participation. In this book recipes from many centuries in the past and many parts of the world have been edited into forms suitable for the modern Western table as a kind of history in action.

1

FOOD *in the* ANCIENT WORLD – TO *the* TIME *of* CHRIST

Bread and manna

Man from the beginning ate grain: bread or porridge were basic to his diet. Manna, the biblical 'bread from heaven', supported the Israelites for forty years. According to the story, the Israelites, having finally escaped from the Egyptians, found themselves starving in the desert. They complained bitterly to their leaders and miraculously the next morning the ground was covered in white sweet-tasting granules – about the size of coriander seeds – which they baked into bread and made into porridge. This manna is thought probably to have been wind-borne lichens which can be carried great distances and, on several occasions in modern times, have fallen in the Middle East. Breads made from a mixture of lichen and flour are still sometimes eaten by bedouin. Back in Egypt the Israelites would have had flat cakes made from toasted grains of barley, wheat or millet. The meal, mixed with water into a paste, was either dried in the sun or baked on the flat stones of the hearth.

Primitive grains needed toasting before the hard outer shells could be stripped off but at some stage the Egyptians discovered a strain of wheat which could be threshed without being toasted. The value of this discovery lay in the behaviour of dough made with raw flour. The early Egyptians must have discovered that doughs from untoasted grains sometimes became spongy so that when baked the bread puffed up and remained light even after the end of cooking. Over the centuries they also discovered how to ferment beer and adapted this knowledge to their bread-making. Egyptian bread was said to have a sour taste which suggests they used either lees of beer or possibly a sour dough for their leaven. (Sour dough is a piece of fermented dough saved

Egyptian model of a baker kneading bread around 1900 BC.

from a previous baking and used to start the fermenting process afresh in the new dough.) By the third millennium BC the Egyptians had become skilled bread-bakers.

The earliest Greeks probably made unleavened breads from coarse wheat or barley meal. During the last millennium BC they began to use bread ovens – previously their breads were baked in hot ashes – and leavens to raise their breads. By 500 BC Greece had become increasingly dependent on grain imports including Egyptian bread wheat. The Greeks favoured bread made with wheat, considering it more nourishing, more digestible and in every way superior to that made from barley. They thought barley bread was suitable only for the poor or the 'barbarians' of the north. Bread made from refined flour – that is flour which had been sifted several times through progressively finer sieves removing most of the chaff – was also considered more healthy than that made from unsifted flour. Greek bakers produced a wide variety of different breads.

According to an account of Greek food written in the first century AD, they had oven-baked white raised bread, that 'was so thick that it bulged from the basket' and smelt of honey; hot rolls as white as milk; large unleavened 'dirty' Cilician loaves; light, thin wafer breads baked over charcoal and others cooked on spits. Breads were sprinkled with poppy seeds, sesame seeds and flax seeds and flavoured with honey, cheeses, aniseed or pepper. The Cappadocians (who lived in a part of what is now modern Turkey) made a soft bread from a dough mixed with milk, oil and a little salt and baked in an oven, not so different from modern Western bread.

The Romans also took their bread just as seriously and had reputedly learnt the art of bread-making from the Greeks. A Roman satirist said that if a man devoted one twelfth of the time on philosophy that he devoted to getting better bread out of his cook, he might be a good man. A measure of the importance of bread to the Romans can be seen at the end of the second century BC when the Roman senate started regular distributions of free bread. Already by the middle of the third century BC, in an effort to alleviate the poverty and unrest in Rome, all grain exports from Sicily and Sardinia had to be sent to Italy where they were sold at subsidised prices in Rome. In the following century the free distribution of first grain and then bread was organised in Rome and for several hundred years the city continued to provide

Loading a Roman grain ship, from a fresco of circa *200 AD.*

free, or subsidised bread for nearly a third of its citizens. The free bread handouts together with the gladiatorial events staged in the Colosseum were the origins of the phrase 'bread and circuses'. The demand for grain necessitated the importation of wheat on a grand scale. Officials supervised its transport by fleets of ships from Egypt, Sicily and North Africa to the imperial granaries at Ostia, the port for Rome. Special docks and lighthouses were built for these grain ships and ships' captains were bound to deliver the grain direct to Ostia on pain of death or banishment.

Roman professional bakers thrived; they invented rotary mills powered by animals and sophisticated ovens with systems of draughts and chimneys to control the heat. They milled the flour into various grades, ranging from the finest white to coarse chaff-filled flour considered suitable for slaves. For leaven they used sour dough and the breads they baked equalled the Greeks' in range and variety.

A Roman dinner

The earliest Romans were a rural people and ate country foods; thick porridges of barley or beans and green vegetables with flat barley bread hard-baked in the ashes of the fire. Their cheeses were made from goat's milk; meat was a rarity and fish unpopular. They flavoured their foods with garlic, parsley, olives and olive oil, all native plants.

By the first century BC the power of Rome had spread around the Mediterranean. Eventually she controlled Spain, France, Greece, Britain, the eastern Mediterranean including Anatolia and Egypt, and all of north Africa. Nevertheless, the majority of people in the city of Rome were poor and their foods, like those of the early Romans, were thick grain soups, often of millet, and coarse bread together with a little turnip or a few beans. Raw olives or goat's cheese or figs added flavour to their diet, helped out occasionally by pieces of cooked pork or meat balls from the reeking cookshops that lined the narrow streets of the city of Rome. The wealthy few, on the other hand, had foods from all the known world on their tables. Spices were carried enormous distances from India, south-east Asia and China. Wheat came from Egypt, ham from Gaul and wine from Greece. Ginger from China travelled overland through central Asia; cloves from Indonesia travelled by sea to Ceylon and then on by sea and land to Alexandria. Pepper from India, the most important

A Roman butcher at work. Behind him are scales and above hang joints of meat.

spice in Roman cooking, crossed the Arabian Sea and was carried overland through Egypt, paid for by Roman gold and silver – to the detriment of the Empire's balance of payments. By the beginning of the fifth century AD pepper was so valuable that 5000 pounds of it was part of the tribute paid by Rome to the besieging Visigoths under Alaric.

Wealthy Romans became notorious for their extravagance and the luxury of their life style, and accounts of gluttonous meals and wild drinking parties still survive. Cicero gave a dinner for Caesar at Puteoli during the Saturnalia of 45 BC which involved him in considerable expense. In addition to a body-guard of 2000 soldiers, Caesar had an entourage of around twenty-seven people. Cicero had to provide three dining rooms each with a table around which nine guests could recline – more standard Roman dinners were smaller affairs in one room. Cicero reported that all his guests ate well 'but once is enough'. Other meals were more frugal and closer to modern tastes. A dinner given by the poet Martial for a few friends started with hors-d'œuvres: a salad of mallow leaves, lettuces, leeks and mint, and two fish dishes, one a lizard fish (a cheap fish) garnished with sliced eggs and rue, and another of tunny fish. The main course included a kid, meat balls and beans, together with a chicken and 'a ham that has already survived three dinners'. The meal ended with dessert of ripe apples and a vintage wine.

Lists of dishes without details of their cooking give only a tantalising half-picture. The only surviving Roman cookbook, said to be by Apicius, is roughly contemporary with Martial's dinner so it is possible to surmise how his dishes might have been cooked. Apicius wrote two books on cooking and sauces and, during his lifetime, had the reputation for being a wealthy glutton. It was said that, after spending a fortune on food, Apicius found himself relatively impoverished and committed suicide. Although not all the recipes in the Roman cookbook are his he was perhaps more deserving of the title gourmet than glutton.

Roman salads were not so unlike our own: mallow leaves, boiled like spinach, were dressed with *liquamen*, wine, oil and vinegar. *Liquamen* was a sauce made from fermented, salted anchovies and used by the Romans to increase the savoury flavour of their meat and vegetable dishes. It seems to have resembled the modern *nam pla* used widely in Thai cooking. Lettuces were also dressed with *liquamen*, a little oil, wine and chopped onions, while leeks were braised with salt, water and oil and then served with a dressing of oil, *liquamen* and wine – close to the modern *à la Grecque* style. Grilled tunny fish could be served with a spiced sweet and sour sauce of pepper, lovage, celery seed, mint, rue, honey, vinegar, wine and oil. Roast kid was basted with pepper, asafoetida (an Indian spice with a strong garlicky smell), *liquamen* and oil before being grilled in front of an open fire. It was served with a final dusting of pepper. Hams were boiled with dried figs and bay leaves – not unlike the modern taste for eating Parma ham with figs – and then baked with honey in a pastry coating, a style of cooking ham still current today. Chickens were roasted or boiled in a variety of spiced sauces. In a recipe for chicken with a peppery cream sauce, Apicius directs the cook to:

> cook the chicken in the following liquor: *liquamen*, oil, wine, to which you add a bouquet of leek, coriander and savory. When it is done pound pepper, pine-kernels, pour on two cyathi [$=\frac{1}{6}$ pint] of *liquamen* and some of the cooking-liquor from which you have removed the bouquet. Blend with milk and pour the contents of the mortar over the chicken. Bring to the boil. Pour in beaten egg-white to bind. Put the chicken on a serving dish and pour the sauce over. This is known as white sauce.

When this recipe was adapted and cooked, it was surprisingly like modern south-east Asian cooking. The sauce was rich with a bite to it and very good to eat. I used a guinea fowl instead of modern chicken for the sake of its stronger flavour and tougher flesh. In the original recipe there seems to be a confusion between the 'white' in sauce and in egg. Egg whites cannot bind a sauce and if they were used as directed in the original recipe the sauce would have a rather unpleasant granular texture. Here is my modern version of Apicius' dish:

CHICKEN À LA VARIUS

SERVES 4

1 × 2½-lb (1.25-kg) guinea fowl
2 tablespoons olive oil
3 fl oz (85 ml) vino verde
6 branches marjoram or summer savory
16 stalks fresh coriander leaves
5 oz (150 g) leeks, sliced
4 fillets of salt-preserved anchovies mashed into 3 tablespoons water
1 tablespoon freshly ground black pepper
4 tablespoons pine kernels
3 fl oz (85 ml) milk
2 egg yolks, size 3

Joint the guinea fowl and discard the backbone. In a casserole brown the joints in the oil and then add the wine, marjoram (or savory), coriander, leeks and 2 tablespoons of the mashed anchovies and water mixture. Bring just to the boil and then reduce the heat, cover the pan and leave to cook gently for $1\frac{1}{4}$ hours. Meanwhile work the ground pepper, pine kernels and remaining mashed anchovies and water to a stiff paste in a food processor. In a separate bowl, beat the milk and egg yolks together. When the fowl is cooked, lift the joints onto a heated serving dish and keep warm. Strain the remaining cooking liquor and if necessary turn up the heat and reduce to 5 fl oz (150 ml) before adding it to the food processor. Work until the mixture is a smooth thin cream. Pour in the egg and milk mixture, mix quickly and tip into a clean saucepan. Heat the sauce over a moderate heat stirring all the time until the sauce thickens and coats the back of a spoon. Take care that it does not boil. Pour over the guinea fowl and serve.

The range and variety of foods available to wealthy Romans continually widened and with the rising standards came a growing sophistication of cookery skills and increasingly discerning palates among the diners. From being a chore, something that the cheapest slave could do, cooking in the second century BC turned into an art. In the last century BC a slave-cook cost as much as a horse and by the first century AD he cost as much as three horses – although this was only a third as much as a really expensive fish.

A great deal of detail survives about the manner of serving and eating Roman meals. The Romans ate three meals a day. Breakfast, eaten some time between eight and ten, might be of bread and cheese or only a glass of water; lunch, eaten at noon with little ceremony, was usually nothing more than bread with cold meats, vegetables and fruit, washed down with a little wine. The serious meal of the day was dinner, eaten around eight in the evening in winter and nine in the summer. It was served in a room furnished with couches and cushions on which the diners reclined – this was considered the best position for serious eating or drinking. Most foods were eaten with the fingers, which were rinsed from time to time during the meal. The diners were provided with knives, toothpicks and spoons of various shapes and a napkin to spread over the cushions. Some diners brought their own napkins and used them as doggy bags to take home the uneaten titbits.

A people apart

Long before there was any Roman Empire, more than 1000 years before the birth of Christ, the Jews formalised their dietary restrictions under Mosaic law. These laws made clear the distinctions between 'clean' and therefore permitted foods and 'unclean' and therefore forbidden foods. Blood was seen as the life force and was forbidden, so all food animals had to drained of their blood – as they are today in kosher ritual slaughter. The distinctions between the 'clean' and 'unclean' followed the known order of the world as seen by a simple nomadic people. Fish that swim with their fins and have scales were 'clean' but shellfish, who have neither fins nor scales but swim in water, were deviant and so 'unclean'. Cows, sheep and goats, all grass-eating animals which chewed the cud and had cloven hoofs, were the familiar domesticated animals of the Hebrew nomads and were 'clean'. The pig, on the other hand, could not live on grass, was impossible to herd and had little stamina for the nomad way of life. Although it, too, had cloven hoofs, it belonged not to nomad Israelite communities but rather to the urban Egyptian and other Middle Eastern peoples. The 'uncleanliness' of the pig was thus a sign of Israelite separateness. The Mosaic dietary laws marked the Jews as a people apart and through observance of the laws they gained both identity and unity.

Jewish cooking throughout history has been shaped by Mosaic law, but it is also astonishingly varied. Wherever Jews travelled throughout the world they adapted the local foods and spices to the ancient laws. The Jews in the ghettos of Eastern Europe adopted medieval central European cookery. For the fish for their sabbath meal they ate gefilte fish – poached fish cakes made with the flesh scraped from the skin and bones and mixed with onions, seasonings and breadcrumbs, bound with egg. Such a recipe belongs to the tradition of a poor people far from the sea. On the other hand the Jews of the Mediterranean lands had fresh fish in abundance for their sabbath meals. They shared the riches of Greek and Persian cooking, lavishly using the fruits, nuts and vegetables of the region in their dishes.

The diet of the Roman army

The Roman Empire depended on the army for its existence. By the first century AD Roman soldiers were stationed on the borders of Scotland, in Germany, Spain, Egypt and on the edges of the Black Sea. This huge army had to be fed and large numbers of Roman officials were occupied in organising its supplies. The soldiers were issued with daily rations of grain or bread, meat, wine and oil and the cost was deducted from their pay. Cheese, vegetables and salt were sometimes included in these basic rations. When the legions were on the march, they carried a scythe to cut crops, a metal cooking pot, a mess tin and three days' emergency food of hard tack (dried cooked grain which could be eaten without further cooking), salted pork and sour wine, a form of cheap wine usually drunk with water. The standard way of cooking meat was by boiling or grilling, and soldiers were issued with spits as standard equipment. A quern to grind flour was carried for every ten men, and a portable oven. Soldiers ate their ration of wheat or barley either as bread or porridge. In peacetime the ordinary soldier was expected not only to grind his own grain but also bake his own bread, either in an oven or on hot stones in the ashes of the fire. Justinian, the soldier-emperor, was proud of his capacity to make his own bread.

In addition to army rations, soldiers supplemented their diet by hunting, or with presents from their families and private purchases from inns or shops

A gridiron found at the Roman military stronghold of Colchester. It would have been used as a stand for cooking pots and dates from the first century AD.

established close to the barracks for this purpose. A letter from one soldier to a friend in another garrison on the Roman Wall in Northumberland asked him to send 20 chickens and 200 eggs as soon as possible – if they were cheap. In wartime, troops foraged from enemy countrysides and at other times the army obtained supplies by compulsory purchases at fixed prices from civilians in the region, by civilian contracts for bulk purchases, or from crops grown on land surrounding the settled army forts. Soldiers made their own cheeses from the milk of animals kept at the forts. Roman army officers in the provinces lived well, eating fresh meat when possible, and enjoying imported delicacies such as edible snails, olives, vintage wines, pepper, fish sauce, hams and oysters. Oysters were a particular favourite of the Romans. By the first century BC they had discovered how to culture oysters in Italy. In south-west France Roman manors had their own oyster tanks to ensure a fresh supply of the delectable molluscs, while for the Roman soldiers stationed on Hadrian's Wall oysters harvested in the river estuaries in the south of Britain were carried north in tanks of water. So highly prized were the oysters from the Colne river mouth that they were even carried in this manner to Rome. The officers' families often lived with them in houses with well-equipped kitchens. A recipe for roasting snails from the cookbook by Apicius gives an idea of the dishes enjoyed by the officers and their families: 'ROAST SNAILS: baste diligently with *liquamen*, pepper, cumin.' The appetising flavour of *liquamen*, coupled with cumin and pepper, might make a very good contrast to the flavourless texture of the snails, just as today we eat them with garlic butter.

The huge size of the Roman army – 300 000 men in the first century AD – involved an enormous organisational job in supplying the garrisons and moving food around the Empire. As the Empire increased in size so the demands for food became more urgent and the taxation system, which could provide commodities or food for the soldiers, more important. The Empire depended on the army for its cohesion, and the successful establishment of a series of supply depots became a crucial feature in holding it together. The taxation and economic system needed to feed and supply so great an army had a strong bearing on the political structures of the Empire. In time the sole purpose of these political structures as they existed was to channel food, money and resources from the peasantry to the army. As the organisation broke down so did the Roman Empire.

Chinese food in the last millennium BC

While classical Greece and Rome flourished in Europe, in the East China was emerging into the full light of written history. Ancient China was a northern land of harsh winters and alternate drought and flood in summer. Her traditional grain foods were millet, wheat, barley and soya beans – rice grew only in the south and was carried north for the Imperial court. Grains were cooked whole in ancient China, for flour milling did not come into general use until around the first century AD. A court banquet some time around the sixth century BC included roast turtle and fresh fish, bamboo shoots and reed tips, but the mass of the people lived on a diet dominated by beans and grains flavoured with sour or bitter herbs.

Salt and sour plums were the earliest seasonings used, but by the fifth century BC Chinese cooks had a choice of herbs and pickled meats for bitter flavours, honey and maltose from grains for sweet, and prickly ash, mustard or ginger for hot, although the latter may have been as bitter as it was hot. Around the second century BC fermented, salted soya beans became very popular and were produced on a commercial scale – in a large city a man could live like 'a lord of a thousand chariots' if he made 600 gallons of salted beans annually. It was, however, another 400 years or so before soy sauce arrived.

The Chinese around the time of Christ knelt on mats or flat cushions to eat, rather in the manner still used at traditional Japanese meals. The food was laid out in front of the diners either on the floor or on low tables. At this time chopsticks were just becoming widely used, although people still ate soup stews with spoons and possibly grains such as rice or millet with their fingers.

Right: A tomb illustration from north-east China showing the preparation of a banquet in the kitchen quarters of a great Chinese house around AD 200. At the top, various animals, fish and birds hang from a meat rack. Below, servants prepare individual tables, cooks slice fish and meat while others thread meats onto skewers and grill kebabs. To the left, servants draw water from the well, chop wood and tend the stove on which boils a huge pot. On the right, others are slaughtering animals and a dog has an eye on a basket of birds. At the bottom, pickles and wine are prepared and fermented in huge jars and a servant is chastised.

A book of rules for the ordering of the Imperial household, dating from some time during the last thousand years BC, gives an idea of the table manners of that time:

> Do not roll the rice into a ball; do not bolt down the various dishes; do not swill down [the soup]. Do not make a noise eating; do not crunch the bones with the teeth; do not put back fish you have been eating; do not throw the bones to the dogs; do not snatch [at what you want]; ... do not keep picking the teeth...

Everybody, both rich and poor, ate 'soup stews'. For the rich there were beef soups seasoned with sour plums, pickled meat sauce and vinegar; others of venison, salted fish, bamboo shoots and rice; and simpler soups of beef or dog and turnip. The nobility considered soups made only with meat particularly suitable for visitors. The poor had soups made of vegetables and grain without meat. The Marquis of Weichi and his wife, entertaining an Imperial minister in about 150 BC, 'bought plenty of beef and wine and spent the night cleaning and sweeping their house ready for the feast'. The beef would probably have been made into a soup. But the feast had an uneasy start, for 'early the next morning they posted attendants outside the gate to keep a look-out for the minister, but, although they waited until noon, he did not come'. On inquiry, he was discovered to be still in bed; however, once the feast got going 'he stayed and drank until nightfall, when he went cheerfully away'.

Unfortunately there are no surviving recipes for the soup stews of that time, but one dating from the sixth century AD appears to continue the traditional style. Pork and goat meat are boiled in water, to which is added steamed taro, onions, rice, salt, fermented bean paste, vinegar and ginger. In my version, in place of taro you could use white-fleshed yam or even potatoes, adjusting the cooking times accordingly. You can purchase taro, rice vinegar and red vinegar in a Chinese grocer's. Miso is Japanese soya bean paste which can be obtained in some Western health-food shops.

SOUR TARO SOUP STEW

SERVES 4 TO 6 PEOPLE

---

7 oz (200 g) pork, cut into ½-inch (1-cm) threads

---

7 oz (200 g) lean lamb, cut into ½-inch (1-cm) threads

---

7 oz (200 g) taro, peeled, and cut into 1-inch (2½-cm) cubes

3½ pints (2 litres) water

---

1 tablespoon miso

---

1 teaspoon peeled and grated fresh ginger

---

1 teaspoon salt

---

4 tablespoons rice

---

5 oz (150 g) spring onions, finely chopped

---

1 tablespoon rice vinegar

Red vinegar to serve

Simmer all the meat in the water for 1 hour and meanwhile steam the taro until soft, about 1 hour. Season the meat and its liquid with the miso, ginger, and salt. Then add the rice. Continue to simmer for another 30 minutes before adding the taro. Just before serving add the chopped spring onion and rice vinegar. Serve very hot with a small dish of vinegar, preferably red, at the side as a dip.

When cooked, this dish tasted strongly of mutton. Its flavour seemed old-fashioned, lacking any of the clear, fresh tastes we in the West associate with modern Chinese cooking. However, rather frowsty flavours like this are still common in restaurants in small towns in China, where oils are not necessarily fresh and flavourings limited.

Medicine in the ancient world

Hippocrates, a Greek philosopher born on the island of Cos in 460 BC, first made the distinction between philosophy and medicine. Up to his time medicine had been entirely theoretical with no reference to the actual state of the patient but Hippocrates suggested a way forward using scientific observations of the patient's symptoms as an aid to treatment. He is still spoken of as the 'father of modern medicine'. As a physician he used few drugs, saying 'our natures are the physicians of our diseases', but he paid close attention to the diet of his patients. The teachings of Galen, another Greek doctor living some 500 years after Hippocrates, followed the doctrine of 'humours' – that the body was composed of blood, phlegm, yellow bile, and black bile. This belief, which had been evolving among Greek philosophers for many centuries, was founded on the idea that the universe and everything in it was composed of the four elements – fire, air, earth and water – and four qualities – heat, cold, moisture and dryness – and treatment for bodily disorders should be based upon the strength and interaction of these elements and qualities. The theory of 'humours' was the foundation of most Western medical thought until the seventeenth century.

Indian philosophers developed a humoral belief very close to that of the

A sixteenth-century woodcut showing the four humours: (From left to right) choleric man is hot and dry; sanguine man, hot and moist; phlegmatic, cold and moist; and melancholy, cold and dry.

Greeks. They also stressed the importance of food for the uplifting of the soul and the health of the body: 'All who live on this earth have to subsist on food'. They assigned warming and cooling qualities to all foods. Spices such as cloves and cinnamon were considered warming; coriander and cumin, cooling. They added another dimension to the humoral belief in their emphasis on the importance of purity. The notion of the pure and impure existed in Indian philosophy from the earliest Aryan times. Rice and honey came to be considered purer than other foods.

Ancient Indian food

The Indus valley – now part of Pakistan – was the centre of a flourishing civilisation around 2000 BC. But during the second millennium BC it was virtually destroyed by Aryan invaders. They came from Iran and Afghanistan, driving fast chariots and speaking Sanskrit, a language which shares roots with Latin and Greek. The Aryans were warrior nomads whose main source of food and wealth was their cattle. Their history is enshrined in the sacred Veda hymns, handed down (it is believed) with great accuracy by Brahmin priests for about thirty generations before being written in the fourteenth century AD.

The Aryans apparently had little or no knowledge of spices or even salt when they first arrived in India. They lived primarily on the meat and milk products from their cattle. Barley was their staple grain; ground into flour it was baked into cakes, perhaps the forerunners of chapatis, to be eaten with clarified butter. Crushed toasted barley was mixed into a gruel with curds, clarified butter and milk. Food was eaten by hand. Thick gruels were licked off the fingers, thin ones drunk from bowls or cups made of clay or – for the rich – of gold or copper.

The surviving earlier inhabitants of the Indus valley were gradually driven south across the Vindhya range of mountains which were never crossed by the Aryans. Contacts between the Aryans and the indigenous peoples introduced the Aryans to local food crops and gradually they adopted rice, wheat and beans and learnt the use of spices including turmeric, long peppers (pepper from vines related to black pepper and with a similar flavour), sour oranges and sesame, although they continued to use clarified butter for cooking. As cattle farmers the Aryans had plenty of milk, and curded milk and clarified butter were both ways of preserving it in a hot climate. Rice was cooked with mung beans into a thick gruel or *khichri* and used in the daily offerings to the gods. Other food offerings included rice-flour pancakes baked in clarified butter and sweetened with honey, and rice cooked with milk. They ate the local leaf vegetables and gourds both cooked and raw. Raw ginger was eaten after meals as a digestive. The juice of the soma plant, whose origins are unknown today but which probably belonged to the hemp family, was mixed with rice or curds. It was considered pure and purifying, and inspired confidence and courage, giving powers of eloquence.

One dish still made in India and said to date from Aryan times is a sweet rice cooked in milk and flavoured with sesame. It is like a traditional British rice pudding but rather sweeter.

Methods of growing rice have remained unchanged since earliest times. This nineteenth-century Indian manuscript shows ploughing with water-buffaloes, irrigation ditches, planting the rice seedlings, the flooded seed-beds and harvesting the grain.

SESAME RICE

SERVES 4
1 pint (600 ml) milk
1½ oz (40 g) short-grain rice, well washed
2 tablespoons sesame seeds
3 tablespoons honeycomb or honey

Rinse out a heavy saucepan with water and, without drying it, pour in the milk. Bring to the boil and add the well-washed rice. Simmer over a low heat for 2 hours stirring occasionally until the mixture is very thick. While the rice is cooking, toast the sesame seeds in a dry pan over a moderate heat until they start to dance. Then tip them out onto a flat surface and crush them with a rolling pin. Reserve until required. When the milk and rice is really thick, stir in the honeycomb and continue cooking over an increased heat for another 20 minutes, stirring regularly. Take care it does not burn at the bottom. Lift from the heat and stir in the crushed sesame seeds. Serve either hot or cold.

By the ninth century BC the Aryans were no longer pastoralists dependent on their cattle. They had become farmers. Their needs and foods were listed in the words of a contemporary prayer which asked for 'milk, sap, clarified butter, honey, eating and drinking at the common table, ... freedom from hunger, rice, barley, sesame, kidney beans, vetches, wheat lentils, millet, and wild rice...'

Hindu food and purity

The early Aryans were a tribal people whose society was divided into classes (castes), which relate to the modern castes in India. The brahmins were, and still are, considered the highest caste, then comes the *kshatriya* or soldier caste, next the *vaisya* or trader caste, and finally the lowest or *sudra* caste. To guard and maintain their caste status the brahmins had strict rules of purity, many

A Hindu kitchen – the painting probably dates from the early nineteenth century. Among other activities, cooks are grilling kebabs, making chapatis, and frying sweet honey cakes.

of them concerning food. They believed that food could be polluted by being touched by lower caste people or other ritually dirty objects, and such pollution would affect their brahmin caste purity. To protect themselves from pollution they devised strict laws governing the toilet and behaviour of cooks responsible for their food. Brahmins could only eat food prepared by other brahmins. Even today, if they are rich, strict Hindu families of whatever caste employ brahmin cooks to ensure the purity of their food.

Aryan beliefs originally demanded huge blood sacrifices officiated by brahmins, with ritual killings, particularly of cattle. After the sacrifices the meat was eaten. Gradually, a general revulsion grew up against such mass killings, and offerings of effigies of horses and cows made of dough were substituted. Economic pressures of increased population and shortage of land also helped make the cow more valuable; too valuable to be killed for meat when alive it could produce milk, calves, and dung. Reforms in the sixth century BC ended the ritual slaughter and led to a ban on killing cows for food, although according to a contemporary Vedic hymn brahmins were unwilling to give up beef, for 'as long as it puts flesh on my body I shall continue to eat it'.

It was against this background that Buddhist and Jain beliefs spread. Jain beliefs were very austere, with their followers eating no meat, fish or eggs. Today, many modern Indians follow the Jain religion and are strict vegetarians. Other Hindus, also strict vegetarians, follow the early Vedic prohibitions against rank-smelling foods and ban onions and garlic from their ritually pure kitchens. They may, however, have a separate side kitchen in which onions and garlic can be cooked for dishes not considered ritually pure. Buddhism was the middle way between the rich excesses of the old brahmin class and the austere Jains. Buddhists were not forbidden to eat meat, merely to refrain from killing for food. Asoka, the great Buddhist king who formulated laws in Buddhist terms, ruled from about 270–234 BC. During his time vegetarianism was encouraged for all the people; the palace consumption of meat was cut to almost vanishing point. But Buddhism as the official religion of the court in India lasted less than a hundred years before Hinduism reasserted itself in a new form. Some meat was permitted but the cow had become sacred, no longer killed for food or sacrifices. Today in India Hindu gods in the temples are offered vegetarian dishes. *Khichri* is one such traditional dish. This recipe from Madhur Jaffrey's *Eastern Vegetarian Cooking* is typical of this ancient dish.

GEELI KHICHRI

SERVES 6 TO 8

3 oz (85 g) mung dal, picked over, washed and drained
Long-grain or short-grain rice, measured to the 4-fl oz (1 dl) level in a glass measuring jug, then washed and drained
2 [old] five-pence-piece sized slices of fresh ginger
$1\frac{1}{4}$ teaspoons salt, or to taste
1/16–1/8 tsp freshly ground black pepper
3 tbsp ghee or vegetable oil
$\frac{1}{2}$ tsp whole cumin seeds

Put the dal, rice, ginger slices and $2\frac{3}{4}$ pints ($1\frac{1}{2}$ litres) water in a heavy $2\frac{1}{2}$-3-qt ($2\frac{1}{4}$-$3\frac{1}{2}$-litre) pot over medium heat and bring to the boil. Stir once, cover, turn heat to low and cook for about $1\frac{1}{2}$ hours or until you have a porridge-like consistency. Stir every 6 to 7 minutes during the last 40 minutes of the cooking to make sure that the *khichri* is not sticking to the bottom of the pot. Remove and discard the ginger slices. Add the salt and pepper. Stir to mix.

Khichri may be made up to this stage several hours ahead of time. Whenever you are getting ready to serve, reheat it over a flame, stirring all the time, or reheat it in a double boiler. Sometimes adding a little water and thinning it out slightly helps in the reheating process. Put the ghee in a small frying pan or in a small pot and heat it over a medium flame. When hot, put in the cumin seeds and let them sizzle for a few seconds. Now pour the hot ghee and cumin seeds over the *khichri* and cover the *khichri* pot immediately. One minute later, uncover, and mix.

Khichri is the origin of the British kedgeree, in spite of the wide differences in ingredients and form.

2

THE FABULOUS EAST – *from the* TIME *of* CHRIST *to* AD 1600

The life of a Chinese landowner

A sixth-century Chinese landowner called Jia Sixie wrote a manual on the management of a country estate. As well as detailed agricultural advice on the growing of various crops, he included two sections of recipes. From these we have a very clear picture of how food was preserved and prepared and also of the foods and dishes eaten by the northern Chinese gentry of that time. They made their own vinegar, fermented bean pastes and soy sauce. In the winter they preserved and pickled meat and fish, or made them into fermented sauces. Vegetables were pickled with salt, as they are today. They marked the festivals of the year with gruels and packets of grain wrapped in cucumber leaves. They steamed a small bear with onion, ginger, orange peel and salt after it had been marinated in fermented bean sauce. The fat from a boiled pig was skimmed off for use separately for 'the fat is very precious, white like jade or snow'. They made discs of boiled dough from wheat flour, and raised other doughs with a barm of white rice and wine left by the fire to bubble. They spiced their dishes with ginger, rice wine, prickly ash pepper (the *sansho* used in Japanese cooking today), and fermented bean sauces as well as the bitter bark of magnolia. A recipe for oil-cooked duck says 'use a duckling and cut off its head. Pluck and clean it. Mince the meat very finely. Add onion, salt and fermented bean paste. Fry until cooked. Add sansho and sliced ginger. Then eat.' For a modern version try the following recipe. The duck is cooked in its own fat.

This second-century tomb tile at Chendu, Sichuan depicts Chinese diners kneeling at low tables. A bowl, possibly of soup stew, and a serving spoon can be seen in the foreground.

OIL–COOKED DUCK

SERVES 2

---

8 oz (225 g) duck breast, without bones but including fat and skin

---

2 large spring onions, chopped

---

1 teaspoon miso

Pinch of salt

---

1 teaspoon peeled and finely shredded fresh ginger

$\frac{1}{4}$ teaspoon Japanese sansho pepper

Mince the duck including the fat and skin. It is better to do this with a knife rather than a food processor since the meat should remain in separate grains. Put the minced duck in a frying-pan and stir-fry over a gentle heat until the fat runs. Break up any lumps of meat. Then raise the heat and continue stir-frying for about 5 minutes. Add the spring onions, miso and salt, reduce the heat and continue cooking for another 10 minutes. Then add the shredded ginger, and sansho pepper to taste. Serve hot.

The rise of Islam

The Persian court in the seventh century was one of dazzling extravagance and luxury. Unfortunately there are no surviving recipes, but a record of the dishes served at the court gives some idea of the sophistication and refinement of the cuisine. Like the Greeks and Romans before them, the Persians paid particular attention to the rearing of animals and birds for the table. They fattened tamed wild asses with clover and barley, and then cooked them with yoghurt and spices. Chickens were reared on hemp, oil and olives and, after they were killed, were hung for two days, first by the feet and then by the neck before they were cooked. Other popular dishes included milk-fed kids and calves, and fat beef cooked in a broth of spinach, flour and vinegar. Game was popular; hares and pheasants were made into ragouts. In summer the Persians ate nut and almond pastries made with gazelle fat and fried in nut oil. The rich had access to foods from both Europe and Asia. Fresh coconut was served with sugar and dates stuffed with nuts. They ate sweet preserves of lemons, quinces, Chinese ginger and chestnuts, and drank sweet wines.

But while the seventh-century Persian court flourished in Iran, in southern Arabia a bedouin tribesman was reshaping the religious balance of the world. Mohammed, whose divine revelations are recorded in the Koran, lived between AD 570 and 630. Some of his teachings or *hadith* related closely to food. Food was considered a gift from God 'so eat of what God has given you, lawful and good, and give thanks to God's favour if Him it is you serve.' The eating of pork, any animal found dead, blood, or animals killed as an offering to a pagan god, fish without scales (prawns and lobsters are often excluded from these) and alcohol and fermented liquids were all forbidden or *halam*. Permitted foods were *halal*. Animals killed for food must be slaughtered in the approved manner; the butcher must say 'In the name of God, God is most great' and the animal's throat must be cut to allow the blood to drain out. These food regulations are still followed by modern Muslims. The prohibition against pork may originate from the bedouin (like the Hebrew) contempt of pigs. The nomad life style of the bedouin in the desert depended on their ability to live away from water. Camels and goats could adapt to such a life but pigs could not.

The bedouin life style at the time of Mohammed was extremely hard, limited in variety and primitive in technique. By identifying some foods in their meagre larders as forbidden and in the self-discipline required in fasting, the bedouins found a new self-respect. The month-long fast of Ramadan, in memory of the Prophet's revelations, is still undertaken for the health of the soul. From the time of the Prophet Muslims have neither eaten nor drunk during daylight hours in the month of Ramadan. Traditionally, each evening after sunset the fast was broken with three dates and water followed, after the final sunset prayer, by a meal. This meal is meant to be of an ordinary size not extra quantity to fill the stomach after fasting. Throughout the Islamic world people still observe these customs although the styles of meal vary from country to country. In Saudi Arabia today people usually eat a meal of bread, milk or sour milk, together with a braised or stewed meat dish. In Malaysia some mosques during Ramadan prepare big dishes of a rice porridge mixed with different kinds of beans, carrots, potatoes, chives, black pepper, fried onions, small pieces of chopped meat and santan milk (made from the flesh of coconuts). This is given in charity to the poor to eat at the break of fasting.

Within ten years of the Prophet's death his followers had defeated the Persians and captured the eastern Mediterranean coast. Arabs who had sailed between the Persian Gulf and India carrying spices for centuries now controlled the entrepôts of Egypt and Persia as well. In the beginning, the life style of the Prophet's followers was harshly puritan. They lived on meat, milk and dates, the traditional bedouin diet. However, as time passed, they came to adopt the softer more luxurious customs and life style of their conquered territories – a life style inherited from the mix of Greek, Roman and Persian influences that had gone before.

The Arab world

The life style of the Arab caliphs who ruled Egypt, Iran and the eastern Mediterranean coast in the thirteenth century was strongly influenced by the earlier Persian traditions, including their cookery. The centre of the caliphate was at Baghdad in Iraq, although their actual power had been much reduced in the previous centuries by the growing independence of the dynasties of military leaders. Trade with the East brought prosperity to Baghdad and the glittering court mirrored this wealth in its tastes and pleasures. Court banquets were famous not only for their luxury but also as occasions for the display of erudition and poetic skills.

A famous Baghdad cookbook, dating from 1226 and known in the West as *A Baghdad Cookery Book*, not only shows the levels of sophistication and luxury enjoyed at that time but also how influential Persian traditions were in the Arab court. Even the names of many of the dishes in the book were Persian. Infinite labour and care went into the making of meat balls, the cleaning and grinding of spices, the condition of the cooking pots and the choice of woods for the fires. The presentation of dishes was important: an instruction 'wipe them with a clean rag' appears at the end of many recipes. The cook was to 'be intelligent, acquainted with the rules of cooking', and 'have a flair for the art'; he should keep his finger-nails well trimmed 'lest dirt collect underneath them'. In the recipes themselves meat, usually lamb, was often cooked with fruits such as oranges, lemons, pomegranates, redcurrants, apples and apricots. Fresh vegetables such as carrots, onions, aubergines, spinach and leeks also appear in many meat dishes. Meats were fried in the rendered-down fat from sheep's tails. Some recipes fried the meat before boiling it. Ground almonds and other nuts were used to enrich and thicken gravies. Expensive spices from China and India, such as ginger, cinnamon, pepper and caraway as well as the local spices, cumin and coriander, appear in most meat dishes. Rice, a luxury in Baghdad in the thirteenth century, was mixed with meat into pilau-style dishes.

A recipe for braised spiced lamb from *A Baghdad Cookery Book* translated by Professor Arberry in *Islamic Culture (1939)*, directs the cook to:

> slice the meat from the bone and chop up small. Cut and slice the [sheep's] tail, and put it into the saucepan with a little water, half a *dirham* of

ground salt, and a *danaq* of saffron: let the tail dissolve and remove the sediment. Now throw the meat into the saucepan on top of the oil, adding pieces of onion, sprigs of mint, and celery, and stir until the juices are dry. Then add dry coriander, cummin, caraway, cinnamon and ginger, all ground fine, keeping back half of the seasonings to put in after the meat is cooked. Then take wine-vinegar, grape-juice, and lemon-juice, mix and add a little of all of the seasonings: if desired a little sumach-juice may also be added. Pour in these juices from time to time, until the cooking is complete. Take out the vegetables; sprinkle with old murri, or if this be not available, then with sumach-juice. Now add the remainder of the seasonings, together with a little pepper. Garnish with yolks of eggs, and spray with rose-water. Wipe the sides of the saucepan with a clean rag, leave over the fire to settle and remove.

Sumach – a relative of poison ivy whose berries have a sour astringent flavour – has been omitted from the modernised recipe which follows. The rose-water used to finish the dish is available from Indian grocers.

TABAHAJA

SERVES 4

1 teaspoon ground coriander
1 teaspoon ground cumin
$\frac{1}{2}$ *teaspoon ground caraway seeds*
$\frac{1}{2}$ *teaspoon ground cinnamon*
1 teaspoon ground ginger
2 tablespoons wine vinegar
6 tablespoons red grape juice

Juice of 2 lemons
2 tablespoons dripping, preferably mutton
$1\frac{1}{4}$ lb (500 g) lean lamb, minced
1 medium onion, cut into quarters
4 fresh stalks of mint
2 sticks celery, cut into 4-inch (10-cm) lengths
$\frac{1}{2}$ teaspoon salt, or to taste
1 teaspoon freshly ground black pepper
4 hard-boiled egg yolks
$\frac{1}{2}$ teaspoon rose-water

Mix the dry spices together. Separately, mix the vinegar, grape and lemon juices and stir in 1 teaspoon of the mixed spices. Heat the dripping in a saucepan and stir-fry the meat for a few minutes. When it has changed colour, add the onion, mint and celery and stir in 2 teaspoons of the mixed spices. Continue frying until the meat starts to dry and then spoon in a little of the mixed lemon and grape juice. Continue simmering the meat, adding a little of the lemon and grape juice from time to time, until the meat is thoroughly cooked and almost all the liquid gone. The evaporation of the juices can be slowed by covering the pan. Lift out the vegetables and stir in the remaining spices, salt and pepper to taste. Turn onto a serving dish and decorate with the hard-boiled egg yolks. Sprinkle with rose-water before serving.

Soon after the Baghdad cookbook was written, Baghdad was captured by the Mongols under Genghis Khan, and much of the Persian-Arabic culture, including the books on cooking, were destroyed in the resulting upheavals. Yet again, a harsher more puritan regime replaced the elegant sophistications of the caliph's court. But Persian traditions in food and art were not entirely lost and returned to flower again in India under the Mughals.

A Persian hunting scene from a late-sixteenth-century manuscript.

Jews in Egypt

Ancient recipe books only really give a picture of cooking for the rich and powerful. Few people considered the lives of the poor worth recording so it is much harder to discover what ordinary people ate. The chance survival in Alexandria of a shopping list for a Jewish clerk's family living in Egypt in the thirteenth century throws an unaccustomed light on an ordinary family's meals. They were shopping for food for the two days of their Pentecostal holiday. In the thirteenth century in Egypt it was normal for people to eat two meals a day, a light morning meal and a more substantial evening meal made up of several dishes. For the first day they bought little chickens, meat, fat tail (from a sheep), a hen, *melokhia* leaves, garlic, sesame oil, and aubergines, and for the second, which was the Sabbath, a boiling fowl, chard, onions, safflower and green lemons. A traditional Egyptian soup going back possibly to Pharaonic times was made with *melokhia* leaves, oil, garlic and chicken stock. Possibly the aubergines were fried in the sesame oil. Most Jewish cooking was done in vegetable oils of different kinds. No cooking could be done on the Sabbath so the dishes must have been prepared the previous day. The foods were expensive so obviously a special meal was planned. The boiling fowl might have been used in a stew seasoned with onions and lemon – still a familiar Egyptian dish – and the chard leaves in either a salad or a soup. Claudia Roden in her *Book of Middle Eastern Food* gives a modern recipe for a lemon chicken.

COLD CHICKEN SOFRITO

SERVES 6 TO 8

1 large roasting chicken (4 to 5 lbs)
2 tablespoons corn oil
Juice of $\frac{1}{2}$ lemon
$\frac{1}{2}$ teaspoon turmeric
Salt and white pepper
1 cardamom pod, cracked

Wash the chicken and wipe it dry.

In a large saucepan or flameproof casserole put the oil, lemon juice, a coffee cup of water, turmeric, salt and white pepper and the cardamom pod. Bring to the boil, then place the chicken in the pan. Cover and cook over very low heat, turning the chicken over frequently and adding another coffee cup of water as the juices are absorbed. Continue cooking until the chicken is very soft and tender. Adjust the seasoning. Remove the pan from the heat and allow to cool.

Divide the chicken into joints, removing the larger bones, and arrange in a deep serving dish. Pour the sauce over it and allow it to become quite cold. On cooling, it will become a pale, lemony yellow jelly and the chicken will be a very delicate off-white. If you prefer an absolutely clear jelly, simply skim any fat off the surface before pouring it over the chicken. Use kitchen paper to remove the last traces.

China before the Mongols

In Song China (960–1279), luxury was enjoyed for its own sake, not just in the Imperial courts in Kaifeng and (later) Hangzhou, but among the numerous officials, merchants and soldiers who crowded into the capitals. They did not care to eat anything humble or unflavoured; the meat had to be rich and delicious. In Kaifeng if two men sat down to drink in a restaurant the table was immediately spread with a main dish and two bowls of assorted cold meats, five plates of fruit and three or five braises. The Chinese were adventurous eaters. In the search for the delicious, seasoning levels were high – sesame, star anise, ginger, black pepper, onions, salt, cardamoms and vinegar all appear together in one Song recipe. Other seasonings such as orange peel, soy sauce, peppermint, cinnamon and liquorice were common. The introduction of a new high-yielding rice from Vietnam at the beginning of the eleventh century meant that in the next 200 years there were few famines in China. By the eleventh century China had become one of the richest countries with whom everyone sought to trade, and with that trade came new foods and culinary skills. From India came the refining of sugar, and black pepper, stronger and hotter than the native *fargara*. From Persia came coriander and pastries 'flour-crisp and oil-fragrant'. In the 500 years since Jia Sixie wrote his manual, Chinese cuisine had made great progress. Stir-frying was a central cooking method, woks had come into common use, and wheat-flour doughs and pastries had been mastered. Beancurd had been discovered and was increasingly popular. Noodles were a common food for everyone, while tea drinking was an art form enjoyed by scholars and the court. Sweet sauces made with fermented flour, like the modern barbecue sauce, were used to flavour stir-fried dishes. Modern Chinese cuisine had almost arrived. Raw meat and fish were both great delicacies, 'the flavours intense and natural'. Still common and popular in Song China were the preserved and pickled meats and fish of former times. Preserved sparrows pickled with fermented rice and then barbecued was a favourite Song dish.

A twelfth-century Chinese riverside scene. In the centre is a tea house whilst to the left and above are open stalls and more small restaurants.

A very typical Song recipe, rich in ingredients but basically simple, is a salad of preserved pork. The pork is sliced and marinated in soy sauce, before being stir-fried in sesame oil. Then it is shredded and served cold with pickled cucumber and radish, seasoned with garlic, cardamom, Sichuan pepper and orange peel and eaten with vinegar. A modern version, which cannot really reflect the flavour of the original because we lack the dried or cured meats of that time, can be made with raw gammon. The cucumber and radish can be bought ready-pickled from a Chinese grocer's.

SONG DYNASTY SALAD WITH HAM

SERVES 4 AS A SIDE DISH

1 × 5 oz (150 g) slice of raw, unsmoked gammon
1 tablespoon soy sauce
2 tablespoons sesame oil
1 oz (25 g) cucumbers pickled in soy sauce and drained
3 oz (75 g) pickled white radish
1 large clove garlic
2 square inches (5 square cms) dried tangerine peel, soaked in warm water
1 cardamom, crushed
$\frac{1}{4}$ teaspoon ground Sichuan pepper or white pepper
3 tablespoons rice vinegar

Cut the gammon into pieces about $1\frac{1}{2}$ inch (4 cm) by $\frac{3}{4}$ inch (2 cm). Marinate the pieces in the soy sauce for 30 minutes, and then drain and stir-fry in the sesame oil over a moderate heat. Cut into matchstick shreds and leave to cool. Shred the pickled cucumbers and radish into similar sized pieces. Crush the garlic clove, and drain and cut the tangerine peel into hair-like threads. Mix all the ingredients, including the gammon, with the vinegar and serve.

A moonlight alfresco dinner in fifteenth-century China. A dancer entertains the diner who sits in front of a painted screen. The table is laid with chopsticks and three main dishes of food as well as various small side dishes.

Buddhists in China and Japan

It is said that Buddhism was brought from India to China by two monks around the time of Christ. They were welcomed at the Imperial court in Loyang and given a temple in which to live. They brought with them the Buddhist teachings against the killing of animals for food. However, prohibitions against meat eating were not unknown in China before the arrival of Buddhism. At least 500 years earlier filial duty had decreed that people must abstain from eating meat after the death of a close relative, and special vegetarian dishes were prepared for the mourning periods. But the underlying concept in Buddhist teaching that life should not be taken for food was new and contrary to Chinese thinking. Slowly Buddhism made progress in China, and from time to time emperors attempted to enforce Buddhist proscriptions against meat eating, but few rich officials ever habitually abstained from meat for theological reasons, while the poor whose normal diet was grain and vegetables had no need to change. Nevertheless, numerous Buddhist temples and monasteries were founded and richly endowed in the early centuries AD, often by groups of merchants or associations, and these foundations grew rich and powerful from offerings and grants. It was customary for temples to offer feasts to their patrons and Buddhist monasteries became famous for the excellence of their cuisine. The cooking followed strict Buddhist regulations which went far beyond the proscription against killing animals for food. They insisted on five colours (red, green, yellow, black and white), five flavours (bitter, salty, sweet, hot and sour) and five styles of cooking (raw, simmered, barbecued, fried and steamed). All these were represented in a temple meal. Dishes were contrived to create the illusion of eating meat. Flour and water pastes were made to resemble animal barbecues; gluten – the protein from flour – was used for both stir-fried dishes and barbecues. At one vegetarian dinner during the tenth century a gourd with its stalk was served on a plate to resemble a steamed goose. By the twelfth century vegetarian dishes 'like in the monasteries' were sold in restaurants in the capital, Kaifeng.

Buddhism came to Japan from China and Korea during the seventh century. An Imperial edict of that time forbade the eating of any meat except by the sick. However, less than a hundred years later chicken and fish were both exempted from this rule, together with deer – called 'mountain whale' to excuse their killing by an aristocracy unwilling to give up hunting. A stricter interpretation of Buddhist law came in the twelfth century with the spread of Zen Buddhism, again from China. The Zen Buddhists tried to re-introduce a rigid vegetarian diet but in this they were not wholly successful. None the less, Japan's vegetarian tradition has remained remarkably strong at all levels of society until the present century. The aversion to killing four-legged animals for food – particularly cattle – remained prevalent among the Japanese until the mid-nineteenth century, when a visitor was told 'The Japanese do not eat cows. Cows do their duty, they bear calves, they give milk. It is sinful to take this milk. The cows require it to raise their calves and because of this they are not allowed to work. The bulls do their work: they labour at the plough, they get thin, you cannot eat them. It is not just to kill a beast that does its duty.' Today most Japanese eat beef freely, although the older generation, and particularly women, still feel a certain reservation against it.

Zen Buddhist influence encouraged the development and formalisation of the tea-ceremony, some elements of which had been current in China 700 years previously. Zen beliefs in restraint and simplicity gave strict rules of formal behaviour to the tea-ceremony which are still followed to this day. Zen temples in the fourteenth century developed a style of tea-ceremony cuisine which was to have a profound influence on both *haute cuisine* and domestic cookery in Japan. The selection, preparation and cooking of food was guided by rigid rules covering the flavour, colour and cooking methods, very similar to those followed in Chinese Buddhist temples. Only foods in season could be used.

Two main styles of tea-ceremony cooking developed. One was at the Daitokuji temple near Kyoto in the fourteenth century and one in the sixteenth century at the Obakusan temple near Tokyo. The Daitokuji meal was served, according to Japanese custom, in individual servings in very elaborate place settings. The Obakusan meal was based almost entirely on sixteenth-century Chinese vegetarian cookery and retained the Chinese practice of serving all the foods in big dishes in the centre of the table from which the diners would help themselves. This style of meal is still served at the Obakusan shrine after an important ceremony or thanksgiving. Such a meal starts with green tea and a sweet cake served according to the formal tea-ceremony style, followed by a plate of cold hors-d'œuvres, and a clear soup with beancurd and ginko nuts. Next comes a number of different foods cooked by simmering – beancurd balls, aubergines, rolls of thin beancurd sheets, mushrooms, bamboo, lotus roots, chillis, ginko nuts and pine needles. After this arrives a steamed dish, followed by a dish of braised vegetables, a deep-fried dish, a salad of chrysanthemum leaves with a walnut dressing, a vegetable stew, fruit and finally rice cooked with a little green tea. A typical recipe used in such a meal might be this vegetable braise which follows strict Buddhist practice and is known as Lohan's delight. (A lohan is a Buddhist saint.) All the unfamiliar items can be bought from Chinese grocers, with the exception of dashi which is Japanese stock. Packets of powdered dehydrated dashi can be bought from Japanese and some Chinese grocers to be made up into the amount required.

LOHAN'S DELIGHT

SERVES 4 TO 6

1 oz (25 g) tiger-lily buds
2 dried mushrooms
1 sheet dried beancurd skin
1 piece wood ears
¼ oz (10 g) black hair fungus
1 oz (25 g) silk noodles
12 oz (350 g) Chinese leaves
1 oz (25 g) bamboo shoots
3 tablespoons vegetable oil
4 squares fried beancurd
1 oz (25 g) canned ginko nuts
1 oz (25 g) frozen green peas
2 tablespoons Japanese soy sauce
1 pint (600 ml) dashi
Salt to taste

Soak the tiger-lily buds in hot water for 1 hour, then rinse and tie a knot in the centre of each. Soak the dried mushrooms in warm water for 30 minutes, then discard the hard stalks and cut the caps into thin slices. Soften the beancurd skin in warm water for about 5 minutes, then cut into ½-inch (1-cm) wide strips and place in a pan of boiling water. Simmer gently for 30 minutes. Soak the wood ears and black hair fungus in separate bowls of warm water for 20 minutes, then rinse well. Discard any hard bits of wood ears and cut into thin strips. Cut the silk noodles into 5-inch (13-cm) lengths with a pair of sharp scissors and soak in hot water for 10 minutes. Wash and cut the

Chinese leaves into 3-inch (7.5-cm) squares. Slice the bamboo shoots into thin slices, about $\frac{1}{8}$ inch (3 mm) wide. Heat the oil in a large saucepan and stir-fry the Chinese leaves for about 3 to 4 minutes, until softened. Add all the other vegetables, well drained, and the soy sauce. Pour in the dashi and bring to the boil. Adjust the seasoning, cover and simmer for 25 minutes. Serve hot.

Chinese medicinal foods

A Chinese proverb says 'you are what you eat'; Chinese attitudes to food and health rest firmly on this belief. The Chinese believe that what you eat has a direct relation to your health, either for good or bad. There has always been a confusion in Chinese thinking between what tastes good and what does you good, with a gradual progression between foods and medicines. A Chengdu restaurant in the 1980s was selling cardamom buns, dumplings stuffed with China-root and fresh meat and ginseng soup with chicken dripping – all of which they claimed to be both good to eat and good for you.

The Chinese held to the humoral belief that the universe and everything in it was composed of four elements – fire, air, earth and water – and four qualities – heat, cold, moisture and dryness. Treatment for bodily disorder was based upon the strength and interaction of these elements and qualities. The basic division of the Chinese cosmos was between the bright, dry, warm male principle (yang) and the cold, dark, moist female principle (yin). The human body was considered to be a reproduction of the cosmos; to be healthy was a reflection of the general harmony among the separate 'virtues', while illness was a sign of disharmony. The human body was affected by heat, cold, moisture and dryness, and these conditions could be controlled by food, which also had the same four qualities. Fundamental to Chinese theories on nutrition was the idea that 'food and cures come from the same source'. Cooling foods such as green vegetables and fruits would be used to treat fevers and rashes while heating foods, such as liver and chicken, would treat debility and weakness. Modern scientific knowledge supports many, but not all, of these theories. The calorific value of many heating foods is high and this, combined with the iron in others, could be of use in treating weakening diseases such as anaemia and tuberculosis. Many 'cooling' foods, such as green vegetables and fruit, are rich in vitamin C which builds up the body's resistance to infections.

Foods were also used as tonics to maintain health and here the overlap between medicine and food is closest. A ninth-century Chinese medicinal recommended recipes for the health of the individual organs: so for a healthy liver, a soup made of dog meat, sour plums, Chinese leeks and hemp was proposed, while for the lungs, a soup of yellow millet, chicken, peach and onion. In the fourteenth century a dietitian, Hu Sihui, was employed at the Mongol court in Peking to watch over the health of the Imperial family. He wrote a cookbook *Yin shan zheng yao* (*Principles of correct diet*) the purpose of which was to inform the ruling family and the Emperor what they could eat in the way of rich foods and wines and also to give guidance to all the other 3000 or so members of the royal household as to what they could eat without impairing their vigour and length of life. Hu Sihui was not himself Chinese but of Turkic origin. His recipes contained many Chinese herbs and ingredients together with specifically Mongol foods and cooking methods. Many of his recipes were for particular physical conditions as, for example, the goat's heart marinated in rose-water and barbecued with safflower intended for a racing heart, or the goat's leg and cardamom he recommended for strength.

A Chinese dog, shown as a food item in a fourteenth-century cookbook.

Many foods now seen as easily digested and rich in protein were classed among prophylactic foods. For example, chicken soups were meant to be particularly good after childbirth. Other 'tonic' foods were of more dubious value. Strengthening infusions and rice gruels made up a large part of the domestic diet of women, who were for the most part restricted to the house by their bound feet, living in an oppressive, enclosed atmosphere with nothing to think about but their health. Tisanes made from ginger (for general strengthening), chestnuts, or salted bamboo shoots and sesame were served several times a day. At other times of day the women of the house drank strengthening gruels. For example, a long bean gruel made with a little salt and ginger was good for both the kidneys and as a cure for vomiting. It was accepted practice to eat that part of the body which required strengthening, so for example a pork kidney gruel would be considered a tonic for the kidneys. A Tang recipe dating from between the seventh and tenth centuries AD used '1 pair of pork kidneys, trimmed and cooked with 2 cups of rice and 2 cups of white of onion and soy sauce. Flavour with ginger and pepper.' Here is a modern version:

PORK KIDNEY CONGEE

SERVES 2

5 oz (150 g) rice
5 oz (150 g) pork kidney
6 large spring onions, use only the white parts
2 tablespoons soy sauce
Salt and freshly ground black pepper to taste
$\frac{1}{2}$ teaspoon peeled finely shredded fresh ginger

Wash the rice thoroughly in several lots of water and drain well. Then cook it in 3 pints (1.75 litres) of water for 20 minutes. Meanwhile trim the kidney and cut into thin slices. Add the kidney, onions and soy sauce to the rice and continue boiling for another 20 minutes. Finally, adjust the seasoning with salt and pepper, and mix in the shredded ginger. Serve hot.

India before the Mughals

Over the centuries the rulers of northern India had come into contact with and been influenced by Persian culture. They and many of their courtiers were Muslim, but beneath them the agricultural masses of Indians remained devoted to the Hindu religion and the Aryan social system and culture.

The great Arab traveller Ibn Battuta visited India in the fourteenth century. He travelled to the capital of the Sultan at Delhi, and while on the road was invited to join the evening meal of a high-ranking courtier.

> ... They sit down to eat and vessels of gold, silver, and glass are brought filled with sugared water .... They call that *shurba* [sherbet] and drink it before [beginning to] eat ... The order observed at this meal was [as follows]. They would serve bread (their bread consists of thin round cakes like those we call *jardaqa*); then they cut up the roasted meat into large pieces of a size such that one sheep makes four or six pieces, and they put one piece before each man. They served also round dough cakes made with ghee, resembling the bread called *mushrik* in our country ... stuffed with a mixture of flour, almonds, honey and sesame oil and on top of each dough cake was a brick-shaped sweet cake made of flour, sugar and ghee. Then they serve in large porcelain bowls meat cooked with ghee, onions and green ginger. After that they serve something which they call *samūsak* [the modern samosas], made of meat hashed and cooked with almonds, walnuts, pistachios, onions and spices, put inside a piece of thin bread fried in ghee. They put five pieces of these before each person, or perhaps four. Next they serve rice cooked in ghee with chickens on top of it ...

This was followed by various kinds of sweet cakes.

Many of these dishes obviously had Persian origins, particularly the *samusak* pastries. The name *samusak* comes from the Persian *sanbusa* (a triangle) and is more familiar to us today as *samosas* sold as quick snack foods in many ethnic take-aways. It is exciting to find the same pastries described in a poem recited at a tenth-century banquet given by the Abbasid Caliph in Baghdad, translated by Arberry in *Islamic Culture*.

Take first the finest meat, red, soft to touch,
And mince it with the fat, not overmuch;
Then add an onion, cut in circles clean,
A cabbage, very fresh, exceeding green,
And season well with cinnamon and rue;
Of coriander add a handful too,
And after that of cloves the very least,
Of finest ginger, and of pepper best,
A hand of cummin, murri just to taste,
Two handfuls of Palmyra salt; but haste,
Good master haste to grind them small and strong.
Then lay and light a blazing fire along;
Put all in the pot, and water pour
Upon it from above, and cover o'er.
But when the water vanished is from sight
And when the burning flames have dried it quite,
Then as thou wilt, in pastry wrap it round,
And fasten well the edges, firm and sound;
Or, if it please thee better, take some dough,
Conveniently soft, and rubbed just so,
Then with the rolling pin let it be spread
And with the nails its edges docketed.
Pour in the frying pan the choisest oil,
And in that liquor let it finely boil.
Last, ladle out into a thin tureen
Where appetizing mustard smeared hath been,
And eat with pleasure, mustarded about,
This tastiest food for hurried diner-out.

Mughal food in India

Northern India was invaded by the Mughals at the end of the fifteenth century. Their leader, the Emperor Babur, who came from Uzbekistan in central Asia, said of the India he conquered that 'they had no horses, no good flesh, no grapes or musk melons, no good fruits, no ice or cold water, no good food or bread in their bazaars, no baths or colleges, no candles, no torches, not even a candle stick.' Babur's grandson, the Emperor Akbar, ruled India when Elizabeth I ruled England. Akbar built the palace of Fatehpur Sikri – soon to be abandoned through lack of water – and established a court life in the Persian mould. Ice was brought from the Himalayas daily to provide cool drinks and, according to a contemporary account, 'cooks from all countries prepare a great variety of dishes of all kinds of grains, greens, meats; also oily, sweet and spicy dishes. Every day such dishes are prepared as the nobles can scarcely command at their feasts, from which you may infer how exquisite the dishes are which are prepared for his Majesty.' The same account includes a list of ingredients for a number of dishes served at court, but no directions for their cooking. Some of the dishes were traditional Indian ones: *khichri* of rice, split dal and ghee, or *shirbirinj*, a form of sweet rice pudding made with milk, rice, sugar candy and salt. Other dishes were obviously Persian in origin such as this pilau called *Qabuli* made with '10 s [ser] rice; 7 s meat; 3½ s ghi; 1 s gram skinned; 2 s onions; ½ s salt; ¼ s fresh ginger; cinnamon, round pepper, cuminseed, of each 1 d [dam] cardamums and cloves ½ d of each; some add almonds and raisins: this gives five dishes.' The small proportion of meat to rice in the original recipe may have been directly influenced by Akbar's personal prejudices against meat. It was said that he 'cares little for meat and often expresses himself to that effect... If his Majesty had not the burden of the world on his shoulders, he would at once totally abstain from meat.' In the modern version of this pilau I have increased the proportion of meat to rice. This recipe pre-dates the arrival of chillies in India from South America, but they must have been first introduced into India some time around the end of Akbar's reign.

QABULI

SERVES 6

9 oz (250 g) basmati rice
1½ oz (40 g) mung dal (yellow split mung beans)
1½ lb (750 g) lean lamb, boned and trimmed
4 oz (100 g) onion, quartered

$\frac{1}{2}$ oz (15 g) fresh ginger, peeled and cut into slices
$\frac{1}{2}$ teaspoon ground cinnamon
$\frac{1}{2}$ teaspoon freshly ground black pepper
$\frac{1}{2}$ teaspoon ground cumin
2 cardamom pods, husks removed and seeds crushed
$\frac{1}{4}$ teaspoon ground cloves
3 oz (75 g) ghee or clarified butter
$\frac{1}{2}$ pint (300 ml) well-seasoned stock
1 teaspoon salt
6 tablespoons vegetable oil
1 oz (25 g) slivered almonds
1 oz (25 g) raisins
1 oz (25 g) finely sliced onion rings

Wash the rice and soak in cold water until required. Rinse and leave the mung dal to soak. Cut the lamb into 1-inch (2.5-cm) cubes. Put the onion quarters and ginger slices into a food processor and work to a smooth paste with a tablespoon of water. Mix together the cinnamon, black pepper, cumin, ground cardamom seeds and cloves. Heat 2 oz (50 g) of the ghee in a heavy casserole and fry the lamb cubes until they are browned on all sides. Lift them from the pan and keep on one side. Add the onion and ginger paste to the pan and fry over a gentle heat until it just starts to change colour. Stir in the mixed spices and continue stir-frying for about a minute before returning the meat to the pan. Mix well to coat the meat in the spices. Add the stock and bring to the boil. Then turn down the heat and simmer for 1 hour, until the gravy is thick and much reduced. Lift from the heat and leave on one side.

Pre-heat the oven to gas mark 2, 300° F (150° C).

Drain the rice and dal. Bring a large pan of water to the boil with the salt. Tip in the rice and dal, stirring all the time to keep the grains separate. Bring back to the boil and boil hard for 6 minutes. Drain the rice and dal well before

The Mughal emperor, Babur, kneels to eat a meal spread out on the ground in front of
him. Among the recognisable dishes are pilaus and a roast bird.

spooning them over the meat. Dribble over the remaining 1 oz (25 g) ghee and seal the lid tightly with a sheet of tin foil under the lid. Bake in the oven for 45 minutes.

Meanwhile prepare the garnish. Heat a frying-pan with the vegetable oil in it and fry the almonds until they are lightly browned. It will take about 3 minutes. Lift them out with a slotted spoon and put to drain on absorbent paper. Next, in the same oil, fry the raisins for about 30 seconds until they puff out and then lift out and put to drain. Finally stir-fry the onion rings for about 15 minutes until they are a golden brown. Lift out and drain.

When the rice and meat have reached the end of their cooking time, turn off the oven and leave the casserole unopened in the oven for another 10 minutes. Then spoon out onto a heated serving plate and garnish with the reserved almonds, raisins and onion rings before serving.

This recipe can be cooked in two parts. The meat can be cooked the day before. In which case, store the meat and gravy in a clean bowl overnight. On the following day soak the rice and mung dal for 1 hour. Place the meat and gravy in a clean casserole over a gentle heat to warm through before spooning in the part-cooked rice and dal.

It is interesting to compare this recipe with a rather prejudiced account by a seventeenth-century Englishman, John Fryer, of a *pullow* in Persia

> which is a general Mess, as frequent with them as a good substantial piece of Beef is with us, and reckoned their standing Dish; which is made either of Flesh, Fish or Fowl as the *Indian Moors* [Muslims] do.... To make *Pullow*, the Meat is first Boiled to Rags, and the Broth or Liquor being strained, it is left to drain, while they Boil the Rice in the same; which being tender, and the aqueous parts evaporating, the Juice and Gravy incorporates with the Rice, which is Boiled almost dry; then they put in the Meat again with Spice, and at last as much Butter as is necessary, so that it becomes not too Greasy or Offensive either to the Sight or Taste; and it is then Boiled enough when it is fit to be made into Gobbets, not slabby, but each Corn of Rice is swelled and filled, not burst into Pulp; and then with *Mango* or other *Achar* [chutney], they will devour whole Handfuls (for spoons are not in use...)

3

THE EUROPEAN DAWN – *from* 1000 *to* 1600

Exceptional events rather than everyday activities make historical records. Equally, in the history of food it is the accounts of special feasts given by kings and nobles which have survived. Throughout Europe, at the courts of great nobles, the celebration of weddings, coronations and other events were occasions of extravagant display, both in the entertainment and foods provided. Abundance of food was the aim in an era when harvest failures and bad weather could bring hunger or even famine to all. Food bought for fifty guests at a London Livery Company's feast at the beginning of the sixteenth century included 36 chickens, 1 swan, 4 geese, 9 rabbits, 2 rumps of beef, 4 gallons of curd and 4 gallons of gooseberries; for spicing the food they used 2 ounces of pepper, 2 ounces of cloves and mace, $1\frac{1}{2}$ ounces of saffron and 3 pounds of sugar. Those invited to feasts not only ate their fill, but were entertained on a spectacular scale. Indeed the quality and delicacy of the dishes may have come a poor second to the razzamatazz surrounding a meal. Jugglers, minstrels, wild animals and actors performed between courses to divert both the diners and humbler spectators who crowded in to watch the proceedings.

The preparations for a feast were elaborate. Trenchers of coarse bread, hard-baked especially for the purpose, were cut into oblongs to serve as plates. Jugs of water and wine stood on side tables. For important diners a broad knife and spoon were provided – forks were virtually unknown until the seventeenth century. The diners rinsed and dried their hands after they had taken their places at table – an essential token of cleanliness considering most foods were taken by hand from the serving plates. The best and choicest dishes were laid

A late-fifteenth-century court banquet. At a serving hatch, dishes are being filled to be carried by pages to the table, which is already laid with trencher bread, soft rolls, knives and salt cellars.

beside the most important guests, and diners would help themselves with their hands from whatever dishes were within reach. Fine white bread was trimmed into finger-shaped sops and used to mop up liquids, including wine. Pottage or soups were eaten with spoons from shared bowls and mopped up with sops. Other meats and foods were sliced and placed on the bread trenchers, together with a helping of the appropriate sauce. Then, held in the fingers, the meat slices were dipped in the sauce before being eaten. Of necessity sauces were the consistency of mustard. At the end of each course the sodden trenchers of bread were collected to be given to the poor.

To mark the end of each course would come a set piece called a sotelty. These were brightly coloured allegorical, political or topical scenes sculpted from a marzipan made with ground almonds and lavish quantities of sugar.

Sometimes they were festooned with banners explaining their significance. A sotelty could represent the four seasons, or the Christmas story with Gabriel's visit to Mary, the angels appearing to the shepherds and the homage of the three kings. On the occasion of Henry VI's coronation in London in 1429 the sotelties all referred to his claim to the French throne – one showed the Christ child on his mother's knee holding out a crown while St George of England and St Denis of France looked on approvingly. When the tableau had been admired and its message understood, the marzipan was broken up and eaten by the guests. In essence a sotelty served as an eye-catching novelty, a demonstration of the host's wealth and consequent power, and a political lesson for the guests.

Henry VI's coronation in Paris in 1431 was followed by a chaotic banquet – according to an anonymous French cleric. From early in the morning the common people had crowded into the palace. By the time, after much pushing and shoving, the important guests had arrived in the banqueting hall, it was already full. Shoemakers, mustard-makers, kitchen boys, wine-sellers, and labourers sat in the dignitaries' places and, as soon as one of them was removed, six or eight others took his place. The food, which had been prepared in the English style by English cooks some four days in advance, was much disliked by the French who reported that even when it was sent to the sick in the Hôtel-Dieu the poor would not eat it.

France was the most important European wine producer in the medieval era. French wines had been famous in Roman times and after the fall of the Roman Empire some vineyards, particularly on Church lands, survived. St Columba, when he set out on his mission to Ireland at the beginning of the seventh century, had with him a gift of wine from Nantes. By the end of the thirteenth century Gascon and Poitevin wine merchants had established a flourishing trade with the new Flemish ports of Gravelines, Nieuport and Damme where they were exempt from some taxes and given the right to sell their wines in the markets. The wine trade between Flanders and the south-west of France continued until the seventeenth century and became an important part of the Dutch distilled spirit industry. Wines were exported to England from France both from the Seine basin and from Gascony. The year's new wines from Bordeaux arrived in England just in time for Christmas. Medieval wines were lighter than modern ones and were at their best after about four months. They were not bottled but stored in wooden barrels until they were drunk. Parisians appear to have preferred light white wines from the Paris basin, which were described as clear and clean like water, of subtle taste neither sweet nor sour. The English liked red wine. One sentence in a textbook written in 1396 to teach the English French ran 'I wish that my agent would buy four tuns of good red wine for my own consumption at the Easter feast'. A thirteenth-century writer said of Paris wines that they would not give you a bad head unless you drank a lot, but the wine from Burgundy, if it was drunk without water, gave you an awful head, while if you drank it with water it was no great thing. It was normal at that time to drink wine diluted with

A fifteenth-century French vineyard where workers dig the ground, train and prune the vines, and pick and tread the grapes. The wine is tasted from the barrel and the price negotiated by the vintner with a merchant.

water. By the end of the sixteenth century wines from the warmer south were recognised as having a higher alcohol content than those grown in the north. It had also been found that these stronger wines could be kept for several years and would improve with keeping.

Simple meals, for both the nobility and humbler people, might be of only one or two dishes, but feasts could have great numbers of dishes served in three courses. At a banquet celebrating the coronation of Henry IV in 1399, among the dishes for the first course was a boar's head with gilded tusks, a heron, a sturgeon and a pie made with cream, eggs, dates, prunes and sugar. The second course was no less ample and included venison served in a spiced wheat gruel, a stuffed sucking pig and peacocks, skinned, roasted and served in their plumage. The third course had more roast birds, quinces in syrup, grilled pork rissoles, custard tarts and pies of dried fruit and eggs.

It is difficult to judge what must have been the taste of these dishes. Although sometimes the quantities of spices bought look enormous to us – one fifteenth-century household used 5 pounds of pepper, $2\frac{1}{2}$ pounds of ginger, 3 pounds of cinnamon and $1\frac{1}{4}$ pounds each of mace and cloves in a year – there are a number of variables. The spices were likely to be stale and weaker in flavour than those we have now, while meats, either fresh or salted, almost certainly had stronger flavours than modern ones. Sugar was very expensive and thought of as a spice. It was added to both meat and sweet dishes alike but probably served more to enhance flavour than to sweeten or, on occasions, to 'abate the strength of the spices'.

Some of the recipes for sweet pies would appeal even to modern diners. Egg custards sweetened with sugar were served with sops of bread, or baked in pastry cases. This recipe for sweet pies appears in a fifteenth-century English recipe book:

> Take fayre Flowre, Sugre, Safroun, an Salt and make there-offe fayre past and fayre cofynges; than take fayre y-tryid yolkys Raw and Sugre, an pouder Gyngere and Raysounys of Courance, and myncyd Datys, but not to smal; than caste al this into a fayre bolle, and melle al togederys, and put in thin cofyn, and lat bake over the Fyre in Freyssche grece.

Called *pety pernautes* – probably meaning 'small provisions' – a modern version of these custard pies could run as follows:

PETY PERNAUTES

MAKES 12 BUNS

Pastry
4 oz (100 g) plain flour
1 teaspoon caster sugar
Pinch of salt
12 threads of saffron (optional)
5 tablespoons hot water
Flour for rolling
Filling
4 egg yolks, size 2
2 teaspoons caster sugar
1 teaspoon ground ginger
4 oz (100 g) raisins
4 oz (100 g) stoned dates, chopped
Lard or white fat for shallow frying

Mix the flour, sugar and salt in a bowl. If using the saffron threads, soak them in the measured hot water in a small saucepan for a few minutes and then bring the water to the boil. Tip the boiling water, with the saffron threads if used, into the flour mixture and mix into a dough. (If saffron is not used add the plain boiled water.) Knead very well until smooth and elastic. Put the dough into a polythene bag and leave to rest until it is cool, about 30 minutes.

Meanwhile prepare the filling by beating the egg yolks, sugar and ginger into a thick pale cream. Stir in the raisins and chopped dates. The mixture should be very stiff.

Divide the dough into 12 equal portions and roll out one portion on a lightly floured board into a thin circle about 5 inch (13 cm) in diameter. While working on one portion keep the remaining dough portions in the polythene bag. Put 1 tablespoon of the filling in the centre of each circle. Gather up the edges to close the pie, twist to seal and break off any excess dough from the centre. Make sure the pies are completely sealed and have no holes in them. Pinch and press into tidy rounds about $2\frac{1}{2}$ inch (6 cm) in diameter and about $\frac{1}{2}$ inch (1.5 cm) high. Heat sufficient fat to cover the bottom of a frying pan by about $\frac{1}{4}$ inch (5 mm) and gently fry the pies over a moderate heat with the pan covered for about 8 minutes, turning them once. Eat straight from the pan.

The sugar, raisins, dates and saffron used in these little cakes were fashionably new and expensive ingredients introduced to northern Europe from the Middle East. However, the pastry and style of shaping these pies is taken from a recipe for traditional Chinese pastries. There are accounts from seventh-century China of sweet pastries being made and sold in the streets by Persian hawkers. Contacts between Persia and the Middle East were close, as we have seen, so it seemed permissible to use this pastry recipe.

Peasant life

The diet of ordinary people in Europe was very different from that of the nobility at court. A fifteenth-century student wrote home that 'we shall dine today on worts [coleworts: a kind of cabbage], garlic and onions, other meat we look not fore', while Piers Plowman in the fourteenth century worried that until the harvest came:

> I've not so much as a penny to purchase you pullets,
> Nor geese, nor grunters; I have only two green cheeses,
> A few curds, and some cream, and an oaten cake,
> And two bean-and-bran loaves that I baked for my children.
> And I swear by my soul, I have no salt bacon,
> Or eggs, by Christ, to cook-up for you into collops.
> I have parsley, and pot-herbs, and plenty of greens,
> A cow and a calf, and a cart-mare
> To drag my dung afield while the drought lasts.
> That is all I have to live on, until Lammas-time.

Preparing for winter in the countryside: killing the pig and storing firewood.
A baker is carrying freshly baked loaves and in the distance can be seen a
hunt with the huntsmen and dogs chasing a deer.

Eighth-century peasants working for a monastery in northern France fared better than Piers Plowman, for their daily rations included wine or beer, pork fat or meat, cheese, dried beans and generous quantities of bread together with the occasional chicken, eggs, pepper, cumin, salt, vinegar and 'sufficient vegetables'. They needed the ration of wine or beer to help digest the heavy bulk of dried pulses and bread. They ate two meals a day, with perhaps two or three dishes at each. With such a diet they would have been windy and bloated and not particularly healthy. But for peasants the feeling of a full and distended stomach after a meal marked a happy contrast to the times of fast and famine.

Pottage – a porridge-like soup usually thickened with cereal or bread – was particularly popular in England, where it was eaten by both rich and poor. A porridge made with boiled ground wheat moistened with milk and coloured with saffron was served with venison at the court of Richard II, while the poor, when they could afford meat, made a pottage of dried peas boiled in bacon stock, mashed and served with bacon. This dish appeared in a fifteenth-century manuscript and is a recipe still familiar to us today. 'Take old pesen, and boyle hom in gode flesh broth that bacon is sothen in, then take hom and bray hom in a mortar, and temper hom wyth the broth, and strayne hom through a streynour, and do hom in the pot, and let hom boyle tyl thai alye homself, and serve hit forthe wyt bacon.'

BACON AND PEA SOUP

SERVES 4

8 oz (225 g) whole dried peas
1 bay leaf
1 onion, stuck with a clove
2½ pints (1.5 litres) ham stock
6 oz (175 g) diced cooked ham
Salt and freshly ground black pepper to taste

Soak the dried peas overnight in cold water and then rinse well. Put the peas with 2 pints (1.2 litres) of cold water into a large pan and bring to the boil. Boil for 10 minutes and then strain out the peas and discard the water. Return the peas to the pan with the bay leaf and onion and add the ham stock. Bring to the boil. Then reduce the heat, cover the pan and simmer for $1\frac{1}{2}$ hours. Check to make sure the peas are completely cooked before removing the onion and putting the soup through a food processor. Return to a clean pan, and add the diced cooked ham and bring back to the boil. Season and serve.

Frankfurters can be used instead of the diced ham, in which case cook them in the soup for about 4 minutes. For this recipe note that you need whole dried peas not the split variety.

Throughout Europe peasants lived and worked on a similar diet of bread, cheese and pork, usually salted. There were small regional variations depending on what was locally available; in northern Europe peasants probably ate more rye or black bread than was common in the south. Often breads were of mixed grains: a Lenten bread was made of barley and oats and in times of shortage such as Piers Plowman suffered, breads were of made of oats, peas or beans. The leaven would have probably been sour dough. The ordinary peasant's bread must have been heavy, hard-crusted and coarse. In England it was usually baked on a hearth stone or in a pot buried in the fire's embers, since, in general, medieval cottages had only a central hole in the roof for a chimney and no place for an oven. In France peasants were often obliged to use bread ovens provided by their landlord for which they paid with a portion of bread dough.

Not only would the coarse bread probably be very unappetising to modern tastes but very few foods of that time would come up to modern standards. Rats and mice attacked the stored grain, weevils burrowed into the dried beans, bacon was rancid, cheese was mouldy and wine sour. Bread was made from rye infected with ergot fungus which brought frequent epidemics of gangrene and madness. Both rich and poor alike were entirely dependent on the foods stored from the previous harvest. There was never enough fodder to keep more than the few animals needed for breeding alive through the winter, so in the autumn animals would be killed off and their meat salted or smoked to preserve it through the winter and spring. Vegetables such as turnips, beans and peas were dried. A bad harvest or a long, bad winter could spell famine for everyone and disaster for the poor. A series of bad harvests occasioned by a rapid change of climate after 1300, brought a general weakening of the population in Europe which developed into a disaster when famine was compounded by the Black Death.

An anonymous cleric living in Paris at the end of the Hundred Years' War, recorded in his journal that by the end of December 1420 the poor ate only cabbages and turnips without bread or salt. Bread could only be had if one went before daybreak to the bakers and offered their assistants bribes of wine. He heard women with no money and overwhelmed by the crowds around the bakers shops crying, 'I die of hunger'.

Food for the townspeople

In the Middle Ages the distinction between town and countryside was not as clear as it is today. London and Paris were relatively small. Within the city walls were private gardens, while a short distance outside the walls there were fields and vegetable gardens whose produce stocked the cities' markets. Townspeople lived much closer to their food supplies than they do today – pigs scavenging the city streets were a source of continual complaint both in Paris and London. Sheep and cows made their way on foot through the streets to the butchers' shambles. Piles of rejected offal thrown out by butchers and mounds of stale fish from fishmongers' stalls littered the streets, while in London the smell from the Fleet river where the butchers washed the carcasses after the weekly kill was the subject of a petition to the king. Town markets with their higher prices and more numerous customers encouraged butchers and fishmongers to trade there rather than in small villages, with the result that people in towns ate more meat and fish than country people. In the south of France beef could only be bought in towns. All food was limited by the seasons.

In the markets the unwary shopper was at the mercy of the dishonest trader. Stale fish was washed to make it seem fresh, joints of meat were padded with pieces of cloth. So bad was the butchers' reputation that at one time they were forbidden to sell meat by candlelight. Bakers and vintners came in for their share of opprobrium – the bakers for selling underweight loaves, and the vintners for adulterating thin French wine with starch or gum and also for making false wines without grapes.

A thirteenth-century housewife buys fish from a street stall.

The streets of Paris echoed with the cries of the hawkers; the call of good cheese from Brie, or the arrival of wine at the river port of Paris. Around the market at Les Halles, merchants were busy from morning to night selling all kinds of fruit and herbs. There were butchers' and poulterers' stalls at the Porte de Paris, near the modern Châtelet, and in the courtyard of Notre Dame. Bakers in Les Halles sold white bread, cooked the previous day, and trencher breads of different sizes from Corbeil, well-browned and cooked four days in advance. Confectioners sold wafer biscuits with a savoury filling, gingerbreads, cakes, and sweet galettes. At the saucemakers' shop housewives could buy ready-made spiced sweet and sour sauces, mustard sauce, or verjus – the sour juice extracted by pressing unripe grapes or crab apples – which added a sour tang to many medieval dishes. As well as selling medicines which they mixed themselves, apothecaries often sold spices, sugar, honey and crystallised fruit.

A prosperous bourgeois housewife did not herself go shopping but sent a servant. Towards the end of the fourteenth century an elderly Parisian bourgeois wrote a delightful book (*Le Ménagier de Paris*) to guide his young wife through the complexities of managing a large household. He copied recipes

A fifteenth-century bourgeois meal.

from other texts and included with them his own comments and criticisms —
a recipe for stuffed, coloured chickens he thought too elaborate for bourgeois
taste. He provided her with sample menus and directions for arranging a big
party. Among his recipes was one for a veal stew:

> Half cook the veal over a grill, and then cut it into pieces and fry in lard
> with a lot of onions already cooked. Then take lightly toasted bread or
> light brown breadcrumbs, they must not be too dark for a veal stew,
> although dark breadcrumbs are good for a stew of hare. Soak the bread
> in beef stock and a little wine, or in a purée of peas. Mix ground ginger,
> cinnamon, cloves, cardamom, colour with plenty of saffron and moisten
> with verjus, wine and vinegar. Sieve the bread and mix it with the spices,
> the liquid from the bread or hot water.

It is all cooked together with the advice 'let it be more yellow than brown'. Finally the seasoning is adjusted with more vinegar and spices to taste. The pea purée in place of stock would give an additional thickness to the gravy. In the modern version of this dish I used raspberry vinegar instead of verjus.

VEAL STEW
SERVES 4

3 slices brown bread

20 threads of saffron

14 fl oz (400 ml) good beef or chicken stock, boiling

1 lb (450 g) piece of veal without bones, from leg or shoulder

1 tablespoon lard or oil

8 oz (225 g) onions, sliced

1 teaspoon ground ginger

1 inch (2.5 cm) cinnamon stick

4 cloves, crushed

1 cardamom pod, husk removed and seeds crushed

2 tablespoons white wine

1 teaspoon raspberry vinegar

2 teaspoons white wine vinegar

$\frac{1}{4}$ teaspoon freshly ground black pepper

$\frac{1}{2}$ teaspoon salt, or to taste

Extra ginger, cinnamon, cloves and wine vinegar to taste

Pre-heat the oven to gas mark 2, 300° F (150° C).

Bake the slices of bread in the oven for about 20 minutes, until they are crisp and lightly coloured. Soak the saffron in the boiling stock. Grill the veal for about 8 minutes to seal it and then cut into bite-sized pieces. Heat the lard or oil in a casserole and fry the onions until they are transparent, then add the veal pieces and fry for a further 5 minutes. Put the ginger, cinnamon stick, cloves and crushed cardamom seeds into a food processor with the baked bread, wine and vinegars and work into a coarse purée, if necessary adding a little of the stock. Pour the saffron stock over the meat and onions and stir in the spiced purée. Bring to the boil, cover and reduce the heat. Simmer for 1 hour. Before serving adjust the seasoning with the pepper, salt, and more spices and wine vinegar to taste. The dish should be a golden yellow colour.

Fasting at the Church's commands

> Thou wyll not beleve how wery I am off fysshe, and how moch I desir that flesch wer cum in ageyn. for I have ete non other but salt fysh this lent, and it hathe engendyrde so moch flewme within me that it stoppith my pypys that I can unneth speke nother brethe.

So wrote a fifteenth-century English schoolboy about his Lenten foods. His feelings must have been echoed throughout the Catholic world, stretching from Spain to Scandinavia and from Ireland to Poland, for, by the thirteenth century, there were 200 fast days a year when meat, milk and eggs were all forbidden foods and only fish or vegetables were allowed. Lent was particularly hard as it came at the end of the winter, when food stocks were already running low. Only one meal a day was allowed for the six weeks of Lent. For most people this was a daily diet of salted fish – stockfish or red (salted) herrings – served perhaps with a mustard sauce. During Lent, the bacon and pea soup quoted above was reduced to one of dried peas boiled in water and flavoured with fried onions.

The rich had ways to lighten Lent. They could use expensive dried fruits such as currants, figs and dates to distract from the all-pervasive taste of salt herring, and during the hungry hours they could afford small sweet morsels of crystallised ginger or candied violets to offset the pangs of hunger. These sweetmeats broke no laws because, it was considered, they were eaten as a digestive medicine not as an ease for hunger. They could also afford fresh fish. Some religious houses even had their own fish ponds, while other great nobles

A series of pictures showing medieval meals: a bourgeois table (top right);
a king's feast (below centre); and a sparser meal (below left).

moved their entire households during Lent to whichever of their estates had the best fishing.

Le Ménagier de Paris has a number of recipes for cooking fish including one for salted fish. In this recipe for squid, the squids are skinned, cut into rings and dried in a pan over the fire before being tossed in flour and deep fried. They can be fried either with or without onions. The *Ménagier* adds that squid served with fried onions and a garlic sauce makes a meal in itself without the need for any other dishes. The recipe for the sauce comes from a fourteenth-century English manuscript, not *Le Ménagier de Paris*.

FRIED SQUID

SERVES 4

Sauce
1 slice brown bread
5 cloves garlic
1 tablespoon white wine vinegar
Salt and freshly ground black pepper
The Squid
12 oz (350 g) big onions
Salt
5 fl oz (150 ml) milk
2 lb (1 kg) fresh squid
Flour for tossing
Oil for deep-frying

Pre-heat the oven to the lowest setting.

Make the sauce first. Bake the bread in the oven until it is crisp. Crush the garlic and put it with the bread into a food processor and work into fine breadcrumbs. Turn out into a bowl and with a spoon work in the vinegar until the mixture becomes a thick paste. Season to taste. If necessary add a very little water to make a thinner paste. Then set aside.

Peel and cut the onions into rings about $\frac{1}{8}$ inch (3 mm) wide. Put $\frac{1}{2}$ teaspoon salt into the milk and soak the onion rings in the mixture. Clean and skin the squid. Cut the sacs into thin rings, sprinkle with a little salt and gently warm in a frying-pan over a very low heat to bring out their liquid. It will take about 7 minutes. Discard the liquid and dry the squid rings on kitchen paper. Drain and dry the onion rings and toss them in flour. Heat the oil until it is hot and deep-fry the onion rings until they are faintly yellow. Drain well and keep warm. Then toss the dried squid rings in flour before deep-frying for 2 minutes. Serve the onion and squid together with the garlic sauce.

The techniques of cooking also had to change in Lent. Milk made from ground almonds (similar to the *santan* made from coconut in modern Malay cooking) took the place of cow's milk for poaching and stewing, and of eggs in thickening and enriching dishes. Oil, instead of butter or lard, was used for frying. Often two versions of the same recipe were given – one for meat days and one for fast days. In the *Forme of Cury*, written in the late fourteenth century, small pies for meat days were filled with pieces of fried pork, chicken and hard-boiled eggs, seasoned with ginger and salt and fried. On fast days they were filled with a mixture of cooked turbot, haddock, cod and hake with finely chopped dates, currants and pine kernels seasoned with pepper and salt.

Medieval churchmen became adept at finding ways around the strict Lenten rules. An account by a member of a visiting embassy of Bohemians describes 'an unbelievably costly banquet lasting three hours' on Palm Sunday in 1466 at Salisbury:

> . . . among other dishes they gave us to eat what should have been a fish, but it was roasted and looked like a duck. It has its wings, feathers, neck and feet. It lays eggs and tastes like a wild duck. We had to eat it as fish, but in my mouth it turned to meat, although they say it is indeed a fish because it grows at first out of a worm in the sea, and, when it is grown, it assumes the form of a duck and lays eggs, but the eggs do not hatch out or produce anything. It seeks its nourishment in the sea and not on land. Therefore it is said to be a fish.

The author was quite right to be suspicious; it was in fact a barnacle goose. Such practices continued for a long time – in the seventeenth century wigeon (a kind of duck) was licensed as a fast-day food because it was a sea bird. In medieval times beaver tails were counted as a fast-day food because, it was argued, beavers' tails were scaly and much of their time was spent in water, hence they could be classified as fish.

Fast or fish days continued in England after the Reformation for political rather than religious reasons. Skilled seamen were essential to the navy at times when there was danger of attack. To secure a supply of trained seamen, under Elizabeth I laws were passed ordering the observance of fish days not only on Fridays but also Saturdays and Wednesdays. It was not until the middle of the seventeenth century that statutory fish days were finally abandoned in England.

The long fasts of Advent and Lent ended with Christmas and Easter. Christmas in England saw the arrival of the new wine from Gascony and ten days of feasting and entertainment. The end of Lent was celebrated with a great feast on Easter Sunday; according to the household accounts of Bishop Swinfield in 1289 a party of eighty ate $1\frac{1}{2}$ carcasses of salt beef, 1 bacon, $1\frac{3}{4}$ carcasses of fresh beef, 2 boars, 5 pigs, $4\frac{1}{2}$ calves, 22 kids, 3 fat deer, 12 capons, 88 pigeons, 1400 eggs, bread, cheese, unlimited beer and 66 gallons of wine.

Eggs in medieval times were a feature of Easter, just as they are today. In the thirteenth century it was customary to give gifts of hard-boiled eggs painted with vegetable dyes on Easter Sunday. These must have resembled the painted eggs which, until the middle of this century, were a part of Easter celebrations throughout Europe. The Easter Sunday meal traditionally included a lamb or kid in many European countries. In Austria before the war a friend remembers being sent to fetch a kid for the Easter dinner from a neighbouring village, and how as she carried it back in a knapsack it 'cried like a baby'. Her pleasure in the roast meat on the following day, however, quite overcame her distress.

Foods from the East

The Roman spice trade did not survive the dissolution of the Empire and for centuries pepper and spices were almost unknown in northern Europe. Pepper was so precious in the eighth century that Bede left his tiny hoard to his fellow

Gathering peppercorns. The European figure on the right tests the quality.

priests when he died. However, by the time of the Norman Conquest in 1066 Eastern spices and pepper were once again a normal luxury of noble households. The Arabs had established themselves in most of Spain and around the shores of north Africa and the eastern Mediterranean. Arab ships were sailing to India, south east Asia and China and, gradually, trade throughout the Mediterranean increased. Venice became rich and powerful, controlling all the sea trade in the Adriatic. She was a centre for much of the trade from the eastern Mediterranean, bringing new foods and luxuries from the East for the markets of northern Europe. At the end of the eleventh century the slow movement of exotic Eastern foods became a flood. The first crusade produced a great movement of men from all over Europe to the eastern Mediterranean: men who had hardly moved more than fifty miles in their lives travelled across Europe and discovered, among other things, new foods.

Sugar was one of these. Since the eighth century the Arabs had known and prized sugar and, in the wake of their conquests around the southern

Mediterranean, introduced its cultivation to Sicily, Cyprus, Morocco and Spain. In northern Europe it was almost unknown until the eleventh century. Minute quantities reached Venice by the end of the tenth century from the Middle East and the Mediterranean basin, but it was the first crusaders who discovered 'a honey reed' on the plains of modern Lebanon, and brought a taste for this new sweet substance back to northern Europe. For centuries afterwards sugar was regarded as a medicine as well as a spice in the West – almost all the supposed remedies for the Black Death in the fourteenth century contained sugar. The spiced sugar confits, nibbled during the long fasting hours of Lent, were also regarded as medicinal. Sugar was very expensive, costing up to eight pence a pound at the end of the thirteenth century – eggs at approximately the same time cost around a penny a dozen – and only the rich could afford it. Some noble households bought almost equal quantities of sugar and pepper, another very expensive condiment, and stored them both in locked spice cupboards.

During the crusades not all Christian contacts with Arabs were hostile. From the Arabs, the Christians learnt to cook meats in almond milk and to fry meat first before boiling it. The custom of cooking meat with fruit, typical of Middle Eastern dishes, appeared in European dishes such as chickens cooked in pomegranate juice or with lemons. Rice grown by the Arabs in Spain became a familiar ingredient in French and English cooking, but it was always expensive, a delicacy more suitable for banquets than everyday use.

The Arab delight in highly coloured dishes was mirrored in the dishes served in fourteenth-century London and Paris. Many recipes give detailed instructions for final garnishes of red or gold. Roast chickens were coloured with beaten eggs and saffron. Meat balls were dyed green with parsley, or yellow with egg yolks. Sandalwood, cinnamon or alkanet (a plant of the borage family) were used for red dishes. Phrases such as 'and saffron to give it colour', and instructions to decorate blanc-mange with powdered red spice, pomegranate seeds and fried almonds appear in the cookery books of the time. From them we can have some idea of the range of ingredients used in the cooking of the rich of London and Paris – rice, oranges, figs, dates, raisins, spinach, almonds and pomegranates – none of which were native to northern Europe, but all of which appear in the few surviving fourteenth-century cookbooks.

Even the names of many of the dishes reflect the Arab influence on northern Europe. *Sawse Sarzyne* (Saracen Sauce) made with rose hips, almonds, shredded chicken, red wine, sugar, and strong pepper thickened with rice flour and coloured with alkanet appears in the English *Forme of Cury*, while *Le Ménagier de Paris* has a recipe for a *Brouet Sarasinoiz* (Saracen broth) made with eels seasoned with ginger, cinnamon, cloves, cardamom, galingale, long peppers and saffron. Pepper, ginger and cinnamon had been known for centuries in northern Europe, but galingale (a rhizome belonging to the ginger family), cloves, cardamom, nutmegs, mace and rose-water, all commonplace in Arab cookery, only became known in Europe after the crusades. The fashion for exotic flavourings continued, a recipe for a sauce of claret wine, rose-water, diced oranges, cinnamon and ginger to go with a capon dates from the end of the sixteenth century.

Perhaps the recipe which shows most clearly the influence of the Middle East on Western European cookery was blanc-mange. Highly decorated, often made with rice, sweetened with sugar and flavoured with almonds, blanc-mange included many of the exotic ingredients fashionable in the fourteenth century. It appeared in many forms in the French, English and Italian cookbooks of the time. One version for Lent did not include the usual chicken but was made of almond milk and rice, another, also without chicken, was elaborately coloured with green and white stripes. An Italian version of rice, chickens and almonds was heavily spiced with cloves and sweetened with sugar. Other versions were decorated with aniseed confits, pomegranate seeds and fried almonds. In the version given in the *Forme of Cury* the cook is directed to:

> take capons and seeth hem, thenne take hem up. Take almandes blanched. Grynd hem and alay [mix] hem up with the same broth. Cast the mylk in a pot. Waishe rys and do [put] thereto, and lat it seeth. Thanne take brawn of caponns, teere it small, and do [put] thereto. Take white greece, sugar and salt, and cast thereinne. Lat it seeth. Then messe it forth, and floish it with aneys in confit rede, other whyte [aniseed confections in red or white] and with almonds fryed in oyle, and serve it forth.

In the modern version given below pomegranate seeds have been used in place of aniseed balls.

BLANC-MANGE

SERVES 4 TO 6

12 oz (350 g) chicken breasts
1½ pints (900 ml) good chicken stock (not from a cube)
6 oz (175 g) ground almonds
8 oz (225 g) risotto rice
2 tablespoons whole almonds
3 tablespoons oil
1 oz (25 g) lard (optional)
¼ teaspoon sugar
¾ teaspoon salt, or to taste
Seeds from 1 pomegranate

Gently poach the chicken breasts in 1 pint (600 ml) of the stock until cooked, about 35 minutes. Strain the stock into a clean saucepan and mix with the ground almonds. Add the rice and, stirring all the time, bring to the boil over a moderate heat. Turn the heat down and continue cooking and stirring from time to time until the rice is cooked, adding the remainder of the stock a little at a time as the rice absorbs the liquid. This takes about 30 minutes. Meanwhile put the cooked chicken into a food processor and work into crumbs. Fry the whole almonds in the oil until they are golden brown, about 3 minutes, lift out and drain. Stir the chicken into the rice, add the lard (if using) and adjust the seasoning with sugar and salt. Turn out onto a heated dish and garnish with pomegranate seeds and fried almonds. Serve hot.

This was a gloriously white dish with a delicate flavour of chicken and almonds, and a texture like a stiff creamy rice pudding. It seems likely that the harder and coarser texture of medieval breads eaten at most meals compensated for the soft 'baby food' quality of dishes like blanc-mange.

Medieval dietaries

In the collapse of the Roman Empire the writings of the ancient Greek philosophers and physicians were lost to Europe. But the Arabs in Baghdad, now the controlling power in the Eastern Mediterranean, adopted much of the Greek philosophy and science. Arab scholars agreed with the Greek systematic approach to medicine, and had translated Greek philosophic writings into Arabic. They combined them with Indian theories on the properties of foods, whereby all foods were classified and used to balance the humours in man. They wrote books on dietetics, stressing the importance of diet to good health. So much importance was put on the influence of food on health that on occasions a doctor would sit at the caliph's table to advise on the healthiest foods.

Early Christians did not accept that medicine was a science or that physicians could heal. They believed that Christ only had healing powers and to claim otherwise was blasphemous. For them illness was the result of wrongdoing – a punishment – and should be treated by prayer and fasting.

The Western Mediterranean gradually re-established itself in the wake of the Roman Empire and at some time after the sixth century a medical school was founded at Salerno near Naples by the Benedictines. To it came scholars from Italy, France and Byzantium as well as Arabs and Jews. Writings on obstetrics and hygiene during the eleventh century were supposedly the work of a woman known as Mother Trot – unfortunately there is no proof of her existence. However, in later centuries women certainly studied at Salerno. By the twelfth century the Salerno school had an international reputation. The Arabic medical treatises based on the ancient Greek writings of Galen, Hypocratus and others were translated out of Arabic into Latin – the common language of all educated people in the Christian world. The writings of Galen, enlarged and refined by Arab and even Indian scholars, had achieved an emphasis on dietary regime that was lacking in the original. These teachings on diet were to have a profound influence on Western medicine.

During the crusades in the twelfth century many knights, homeward bound from the Holy Land, stopped in Naples on their way home and, according to legend, were cured of their wounds and diseases at Salerno. At that time there first appeared a compilation of the dietary precepts of Salerno, the *Regimen*

He apoſteme uent entre leſ narilleſ.rilleſ.
qē polipuſ apele le greignur auent entre leſ nar

le linſil oingnez.Equant leſ burbletteſ creuerunt

Thirteenth-century illustrations from Regimen Sanitatis Salerni, *showing the making of herbal medicines and the treatment of patients.*

Sanitatis Salerni. This book is said to have been written around 1100 for William the Conqueror's son Robert on his way home from the First Crusade. Basically a handbook of domestic medicine, it had a tremendous influence on medical practice in the Middle Ages and its theories were accepted until the end of the seventeenth century. The *Regimen* assessed foods as hot or cold, dry or wet according to the humoral theory and gave advice on the dangers or otherwise of various foods. Fruits, milk products and red meat were all to be eaten with caution:

> All pears and apples, peaches, milk and cheese,
> Salt meat, red deer, hare, beef and goat, all these
> Are meats that breed ill blood, and melancholy . . .

It also gave general advice on a healthy diet:

> To keepe good dyet, you should never feed
> Until you find your stomacke cleaned and void
> Of former eaten meate, for they do breed
> Repletion, and will cause you soone be cloid,
> None other rule but appetite should need
> When from your mouth a moysture cleare doth void.

The influences of the Salerno School and Galen are clearly reflected 400 years later in the writings of the English physician Andrew Boorde. In his *A Compendyous Regyment or a Dyetary of Helth*, he lists suitable and unsuitable foods for different diseases and describes the ideal diet for different types of men: sanguine men, who are hot and moist, should be circumspect in eating meat, not eat fruit – here an echo of Galen who disapproved of fruit or herbs or roots. They must ration their food or they will be fat and gross. Phlegmatic men on the other hand are cold and moist. They should not eat white meats, herbs or fruit, but onions, garlic, pepper, ginger and hot and dry meats. Choleric men are hot and dry and should avoid hot spices and wine, while melancholic men who are cold and dry, should not eat fried or salted meats, and drink only light wines. The warnings against fruit are echoed in the advice given in 1404 to a Tuscan merchant by his doctor translated by Iris Origo in her book *The Merchant of Prato.*

As to the fruit to which you bear so sweet a love, I grant you almonds, both fresh and dried, as many as you like; and nuts, both fresh and dry and well cleaned ... and fresh and dried figs before a meal and also grapes; but after a meal, beware of them. Take melons, in season, before a meal, and cast not away what is in them, for that is the best and most medicinal part. And I will grant you many cherries, well ripe, before a meal; but by God, after a meal let them be. And I beseech you, since I am so generous in conceding fruit to you according to your mind, be so courteous to me as to cast aside the others which are harmful, such as *bacceli* [young broad beans in their pods], apples, chestnuts and pears.

This belief that fruit can be harmful dies hard; there are still many people who believe that raw fruit should not be eaten with a meal.

Home cures

The invention of printing in Europe – at the end of the fifteenth century – meant that by the sixteenth century many more people had access to books. Formerly only the Church or the very rich had hand-copied manuscripts. Among the first printed books were several which dealt with health and diet; one published in 1475 in Italy included an appendix of recipes. A little book published in Paris in 1572 details the measures to be taken to retain health. It is not dominated by the humoral theory of diet and is quite specific in its recommendations. A typical recipe for whitening teeth and 'to hold them in' uses rose-water, sage, marjoram, alum and cinnamon. These ingredients were all part of a kitchen's storeroom and easily available to the housewife. Rosemary was reputed to be a herb of almost miraculous powers. It was used to treat colds, toothache, aching feet, bad breath, sweating, lack of appetite, gout, consumption and madness. A seventeenth-century English recipe for a children's cough medicine makes an infusion of rosemary and then mixes a pound of sugar into every pint of the liquor. For centuries country housewives had had their own cures for sickness, seldom written but handed down by word of mouth – one such was the efficacy of fried mice in curing bed-wetting. As early as the first century AD a recipe for aromatic salts was said to aid digestion, move the bowels and prevent colds, the plague and all diseases. The salts were

A manuscript picture dating from around 1470 showing the mistress of the house brewing a home cure from her own recipe book.

The herb celery pictured in a medieval illustrated herbal.

made by mixing salt, sal ammonia, white pepper, ginger, cumin, thyme, celery seed, oregano, rocket seed, black pepper, saffron, bay leaf, parsley and dill. The making of potions and the treating of the sick were as much part of the English housewife's work in a big house in the country as her supervision of the preserving and drying of herbs, and her work in the dairy. One sixteenth-century cough remedy of barley water, mulberry syrup and honey of roses sounds good, but others were more dubious, such as this eighteenth-century cure for 'the spitting of blood, if a vein is broken: Take mice dung beaten to a powder, as much as will lie on a six-pence; and put in a quarter of a pint of the juice of plantane, with a little sugar; give it in the morning fasting, and at night going to bed. Continue this some time, and it will make whole and cure.'

With the advent of printing, domestic remedies were systematically recorded, not just in books on health, but in recipe books written for house-wives. Gervase Markham's *The English Hus-wife* (1615) has not only culinary recipes but directions on the treatment of common ailments, while *The Queen's Closet Opened* (1669) has one section entirely devoted to medicinal recipes for various diseases, some labelled 'well-tried'. Most of the remedies are herbal. This recipe 'to help digestion' is typical: 'Take two quarts small ale, red mint two handfuls, red sage and a little cinnamon. Let it all boil until half be wasted. Sweeten with sugar to your taste and drink night and morning.' Not so much to our modern taste is the 'special water for consumption' which started with a peck of small garden snails and a quart of earthworms. Books of a similar style, written mainly for housewives with both culinary and medical recipes continued to be published until well into the eighteenth century.

4

NEW HORIZONS – *from* 1600 *to* 1800

Printed books

The impact of printing on the cookery world was immense. Increasing numbers of people were able to read about food and diet and their interest accelerated the speed of change in cooking. Cookery books broke the dependence of fine cooking on oral traditions. Literate cooks, such as Robert May, the author of *The Accomplish't Cook*, and William Rabisha (*The Whole Body of Cookery Dissected*), could enlarge their own repertoire of recipes by reading the recipes of others. Written recipes established both a consensus and a base from which innovative cooks could experiment. They were written not in Latin, the language of the Church and scholars, but in the languages of ordinary people – English, German and French. Not all the authors were professional cooks. Sir Kenelm Digby, Bart., whose collection of recipes (*The Queen's Closet Opened*) was published after his death in 1665, was a distinguished figure at the English court. An enthusiastic cook, he travelled widely in Europe and was also a Fellow of the Royal Society, a scientist, a qualified doctor, and a philosopher. Gervase Markham, author of the extremely popular *The English Hus-wife*, had been a soldier, minor poet and distinguished horseman, before poverty forced him into journalism. Their books were directed towards three kinds of readers: gentlewomen running big country households (particularly in England); the educated amateur or dilettante gourmet; and the craftsman chef.

Through these books we can watch the gradual change from medieval to modern cookery. The recipes in *A Booke of Cookry very necessary for all such as delight therin gathered by A.W.*, published in 1584, are still basically medieval, full of spices and contrived broths such as this recipe for boiling a capon with oranges or lemons:

Take your Capon and boyle him tender and take a little of the broth [in] which it is boyled, and put it in a pipkin, with Mace and Sugar a good deale, and pare three oranges and pill [peel] them and put them in your pipkin, and boyle them a little among your broth, and thicken it with wine and yolks of Eggs and Sugar a good deale, and Salt but a little, and set your broth no more on the fire for quailing [curding] and serve it in without sippets.

Thirty years later a new style emerges. *The English Hus-wife* points the way to English traditional cookery. As culinary changes arrive recipes are not necessarily dropped but rather new ones are added and the older styles receive less prominence. Nor are printed recipe books necessarily in the vanguard of

What' wouldst thou view but in one face
all hospitalitie, the race
of those that for the Gusto stand,
whose tables a whole Ark comand
of Natures plentie wouldst thou see
this sight. peruse Maûs booke 'tis hee.

THE
Accomplisht Cook,
OR THE
ART & MYSTERY
OF
COOKERY.
Wherein the whole A R T is revealed in a
more easie and perfect Method, than hath
been publisht in any language.
Expert and ready Ways for the Dressing of all Sorts
of FLESH, FOWL, and FISH, with variety of
SAUCES proper for each of them ; and how to
raise all manner of *Pastes* ; the best Directions for
all sorts of *Kickshaws*, also the *Terms* of CAR-
VING and SEWING.
An exact account of all *Dishes* for all *Seasons* of the
Year, with other *A-la-mode Curiosities*
The Fifth Edition, with large Additions throughout
the whole work : besides two hundred Figures of
several Forms for all manner of bak'd Meats,
(either Flesh, or Fish) as, Pyes Tarts, Custards;
Cheesecakes, and Florentines, placed in Tables,
and directed to the Pages they appertain to.

Approved by the fifty five Years Experience and Industry of *ROBERT MAY*, in his Attendance on several Persons of great Honour.

London, Printed for *Obadiah Blagrave* at the *Bear* and
Star in St. *Pauls Church-Yard*, 1685.

Title page for the fifth edition of Robert May's The Accomplish't Cook.

progress; they may reflect styles of cookery already well established in the kitchen. During the seventeenth century English cooking developed a unique country style. At the same time in France, a noticeable lack of new cookery books in the first half of the century suggests that French cooking may have remained medieval in essence until the mid-seventeenth century, when *haute cuisine* made a tentative beginning.

A busy seventeenth-century Dutch kitchen. One maid dresses a bird, another threads one onto a spit, while a third bastes the birds roasting in front of the fire. In the adjoining room the diners sit at table.

English country style

During the seventeenth century many new country estates were established by families who had made fortunes from trade along the newly discovered sea routes to India and the West Indies. They spent lavishly on houses, lands and gardens. To match this new and self-confident life style, many farming, gardening and kitchen manuals appeared. Gervase Markham, whose *The English Hus-wife* was published in 1615, also wrote a number of farming manuals. The 'hus-wife' was expected to oversee and even take a part in the daily management of a large country house. She had to know about the management of gardens, a dairy, a stillroom and 'all sorts of herbs belonging unto the kitchen, whether they be for the Pot, for Sallets [salads], for Sauces, for servings, or for any other seasoning or adorning'. Her food should be cooked 'with care and diligence, let it be rather to satisfie nature than our affections, and apter to kill hunger than revive new appetites; let it proceede more from the provision of her owne yard, than the furniture of the Markets; and let it be rathere esteemed for the familiar acquaintance she hath with it, than for the strangenesse and rarity it bringeth from other Countries'.

This was to be the style of English cooking for the next 200 years. Rural in character, close to the seasons and rhythm of the country, the recipes reflect this life. One for 'clouted' cream begins 'Milk your cows in the evening about the usual time'. The cookbooks are full of pies, puddings, boiled and roast meats and conserves. But the medieval styles of cooking were not yet quite abandoned; a white broth in *The English Hus-wife* which includes spinach, endive, beef marrow, cloves, mace, white wine, ginger, ground almonds, currants, raisins, prunes, and cinnamon echoes the 'white bruets' of the fifteenth century. Some of the fruit pies are delicious, like this one for a 'Warden pie'.

Take of the fairest and best Wardens (pears), and pare them and take out the hard chores on the top and cut the sharpe ends at the bottome flat; then boyle them in White wine and sugar, until the sirrup grow thicke: then take the Wardens, from the sirrup into a cleane dish, and let them coole; then set them into the coffin, and prick cloves in the tops, with whole sticks of cinnamon, and great store of sugar, as for pippins, then cover it, and onely reserve a vent hole, so set it in the oven and bake it: when it is bak't, draw it forth, and take the first sirrup in which the Wardens were boyled, and taste it, and if it be not sweet enough, then put in more sugar and some Rose water, and boyle it againe a little, then powre it in at the vent hole and shake the pie well; then take sweet butter and rose water, melted and with it annoint the pie lid all over, and then strow upon it store of sugar and so set it into the oven againe a little space and then serve it up.

WARDEN PIE

SERVES 4

6–8 Conference pears, depending on size

---

1 pint (600 ml) very sweet white wine, such as a Spanish moscatel

---

Shortcrust pastry to line and cover a deep 1 pint (600 ml) pie dish

---

3 cloves

1½-inch (4-cm) cinnamon stick

---

1 tablespoon sugar

¼ teaspoon rose-water (bought in an Indian grocer's)

Sugar to taste

½ oz (15 g) butter

---

3 drops rose-water

1–2 tablespoons caster sugar

Pre-heat the oven to gas mark 7, 425°F (220°C). Peel the pears, cut out the hard cores at the wide ends and pull off the stalks. Simmer them in the wine until they are soft, then lift them out and leave to cool. Reserve the syrup.

Line the pie dish with half the pastry and roll out the remaining half for a top to cover the pie. When the pears are cool enough, arrange them upright in the lined pie dish. If necessary trim off their tops. Add the cloves, cinnamon and 1 tablespoon of sugar. Cover the pie with the prepared top. Cut a fairly big hole in the centre of the crust and bake for 25 minutes.

Warm 7 fl oz (200 ml) of the reserved syrup, add the ¼ teaspoon rose-water and sugar to taste. Gently melt the butter in a separate pan and add the 3 drops of rose-water. When the pie is cooked pour the prepared syrup in through the centre vent hole, tipping the pie gently to allow the syrup to run to all parts. Paint the pie top with the melted butter and rose-water. Sprinkle over the caster sugar and place under a hot grill for about a minute to melt the sugar. As the sugar burns very quickly, it must be watched.

French courtly cooking

It was not until the middle of the seventeenth century that La Varenne published *Le Cuisinier François*, the first French cookery book to break with medieval traditions. Little is known of La Varenne personally – even his name is a pseudonym. He was a professional cook who worked for the Marquis d'Uxelles after whom he named his most famous innovation of chopped mushrooms seasoned with herbs and shallots. The cuisine which emerges in La Varenne's book is ordered and restrained compared to the former riotous profusion. It is based on a series of techniques governed by rules: basic preparations – bouillon and roux, the use of bouquet garni, egg whites for clearing consommé, and stuffings made with mushrooms and other vegetables – all appear in the *Le Cuisinier François*. Gone are the multi-flavoured sauces and the exotic game birds, and in their place are slow-cooked pieces of beef or mutton. The beginnings of French *haute cuisine* are assembling although not yet complete. The essence of medieval cookery lay in mixture; the cookery emerging in the eighteenth century preferred the infusion of carefully selected flavours.

Both old and new styles co-exist in La Varenne. His recipe for stuffed turkey with raspberries has a mixture of flavours not likely to appeal to modern palates, although turkeys themselves were only introduced into Europe from America during the sixteenth century. But his recipe for *boeuf à la mode*, in which beef is larded and slowly cooked in stock with a bouquet garni and spices before being served in its own gravy, differs little from its modern counterpart. More cookery books followed *Le Cuisinier François*, reinforcing the move in France towards discipline and restraint in cookery. One cookery writer said that soups should taste simply of their ingredients. Butter was increasingly used as a medium for cooking. The flavour of butter and other fats such as goose dripping replaced vinegar and verjuice in sauces, and herbs, especially parsley and thyme, were used instead of spices.

A recipe from *Le Cuisinier François* for soles stuffed with sorrel admirably demonstrates the new style of cooking:

> Wash and paint the soles with butter. Then put them over a grill with a little farce . . . To make your farce, take sorrel, parsley, and raw egg yolks. Chop up the herbs, mix them and season with a little thyme, then put it

into your soles. Make a sauce using butter, salt, vinegar, pepper, chives and parsley, cook it in a pan until very creamy. Serve with a little nutmeg grated over.

The sauce in this recipe appears to be a form of *beurre blanc* – a sauce usually attributed to a nineteenth-century chef. Fish stuffed with sorrel is a continuing French tradition (Jane Grigson has a shad cooked in this way in her *Fish cookery*). The following is a modernised version of La Varenne's sole. Any flat fish could be used in place of sole and, if necessary, substitute more spinach and a touch of lemon juice for the sorrel, which is not always easy to find.

SOLES STUFFED WITH SORREL

SERVES 4

4 small soles
6 oz (175 g) sorrel
6 oz (175 g) spinach
1 tablespoon chopped fresh parsley
1 teaspoon chopped fresh thyme
2 egg yolks, beaten
Salt and freshly ground black pepper
2 oz (50 g) butter
A little grated nutmeg
Sauce
3 tablespoons wine vinegar (red or white)
1 tablespoon finely chopped fresh chives
1 tablespoon chopped fresh parsley
3 oz (75 g) chilled butter, cut into 15 pieces
Salt and freshly ground black pepper

Pre-heat the oven to gas mark 5, 375°F (190°C). Clean and wash your fish. Make an incision across the body behind the head on the dark side of the fish. Then cut from your incision down the centre of the fish along the line of the back bone. Slide the knife sideways from the back bone towards one edge of the fish to free the flesh from the ribs and make a pocket. Repeat moving the other way from the back bone to the edge of the fish. Wash the sorrel and spinach and tear out the central stalks. Dry well, either in a cloth or a lettuce spinner. Put into a food processor with the parsley, thyme and egg yolks and work into a purée. Season to taste. Spoon the mixture into the pockets in each fish. Butter a large ovenproof dish with half the butter and arrange the fish, sorrel side up, in the dish. Dot with the remaining butter and bake until the fish are cooked, about 20 minutes depending on size.

To make the sauce put the vinegar with the chives and parsley in a small saucepan and boil gently until about 1 tablespoon of liquid remains. Remove from the heat and allow to cool for a minute before beating in 2 pieces of the chilled butter. Return to a very low heat and continue beating and adding the butter, piece by piece, until it has all been absorbed and the sauce is thick and creamy. Remove from the heat and season to taste. When the fish is cooked, serve on a hot plate with a little grated nutmeg and the sauce.

The cookery outlined in books such as *Le Cuisinier François* was that of the court. Many of the great aristocracy lived permanently at the royal court of Versailles and took little interest in their estates in the country. French *haute cuisine* as it developed in the eighteenth century was designed to appeal to aristocrats tied to a court which actively discouraged contacts with the country – banishment from court to the country was a punishment – and the aristocrats prided themselves on the expense and lavishness of their chefs' cooking. So contemporary French cookbooks mirrored experiences at court rather than those of country estates, in contrast to England where most of the nobility still lived on their estates. Social conditions in France had produced a rigid social system with little transference from one class to another. As a result many wealthy families, cut off from social advancement by the system, wished to imitate the manners and habits prevailing in the inaccessible higher classes. It was for these people, or rather their cooks, that the French cookbooks of the seventeenth century were written. The fashionable meal in Molière's *Le bourgeois gentilhomme* of a breast of mutton stuffed with parsley; a loin of veal, white and delicate as almond paste; partridges cunningly seasoned; a second course of a rich soup, a young plump turkey and pigeons garnished with white onions and chicory was exactly in the style of these cookbooks.

Laden tables at a court banquet given by Louis XIII of France at Fontainebleau in 1633.

The favourite wines of the rich in Paris during the second half of the seventeenth century were from Champagne. Champagne wines had first been recognised as great wines under Henry IV of France at the beginning of the century, but at that time their capacity to form a sparkling wine had not been appreciated. Champagne was considered remarkable because, although made from black grapes, it produced a 'grey wine'. During the second half of the same century Dom Pérignon, a monk at the Abbey of Hautvillers near Rheims had charge of the vineyards, wine presses and cellars at the abbey. He became renowned as a great wine master and it was said that his outstanding skill in choosing vines, in pruning and in blending the grapes was responsible for the excellence of the wine from the abbey. Even in his very last years as an old man he could place the provenance of any grape he tasted.

The delicate flavour of Champagne was quickly lost when the wine was stored in wooden barrels, but it was found that in tightly stoppered glass bottles it could keep its flavour for up to six years. When it was stored in this way it also fermented again and became sparkling. Mistakenly, it has sometimes been claimed that Dom Pérignon introduced the use of corks for glass wine bottles in place of the old-style wooden stoppers bound round with string which did not always give a tight enough seal for sparkling wine. Although Pérignon was responsible, with others, for perfecting the wines of the province, the technique now called *méthode champenoise* was not devised in his lifetime.

Champagne was the most popular wine at the English court of Charles II where it was especially praised for its sparkling quality. In the beginning the sparkling of champagne was not much admired in France but by the end of the century French wine drinkers came to prize this characteristic as much as the English did.

There were at that time no *appellation contrôlée* or great vintage wines. Claret, imported in barrels from Bordeaux, was light in colour and of uneven quality. It was usually drunk warmed with spices as mulled wine. Younger wines were more expensive than older wines, because wines kept in barrels tended to go

Corkscrews have not changed much since their first appearance in the eighteenth century.

off after a year or so. Gradually during the eighteenth century, as blown glass bottles and cork stoppers became more common, it was discovered that other wines, as well as champagne, improved with keeping in the bottle. Slowly after the French Revolution some wine growers took steps to improve and protect the quality of their wines. Some of the great châteaux started to bottle their own wines, thus ensuring the quality of the wine carrying their name and introducing a system of named vineyards. In 1855 the earliest classification system was introduced in the Bordeaux region, although it had no legal status until the twentieth century.

Meals and mealtimes

On 13 January 1663 Samuel Pepys gave a dinner party. Pepys at this time was Secretary to the Navy and an important man. He had a house at the Navy Office in Seething Lane near Tower Hill. On the 13th he wrote:

> ... my poor wife rose by 5 a-clock in the morning, before day, and went to market and bought fowle and many other things for dinner – with which I was highly pleased. And the chine of beef was down also before 6 a-clock, and my own Jacke [for roasting], of which I was doubtful, doth carry it very well. Things being put in order and the Cooke come, I went to the office, where we sat till noon; and then broke up and I home – whither by and by comes Dr. Clerke and his lady – his sister and a she-Cosen, and Mr. Pierce and his wife, which was all my guest[s].
>
> I had for them, after oysters – at first course, a hash of rabbits and lamb, and a rare chine of beef [that had been roasted] – next, a great dish of roasted fowl, cost me about 30s and a tart; and then fruit and cheese. My dinner was noble and enough.

The guests evidently stayed the rest of the day playing cards and talking, for 'At night to supper; had a good sack-posset and cold meat and sent my guests away about 10 a-clock at night – both them and myself highly pleased with our management of this day.'

A contemporary recipe for hashed rabbits appears in Robert May's *The Accomplish't Cook* which was first published in 1660. Perhaps it is not too fanciful to imagine that Pepys's cook took:

a rabit being flayed and wiped clean; then cut off the thighs, legs, wings [!] and head, and part the chine into four pieces, put all into a dish or pipkin, and put to it a pint of white wine, and as much fair water, gross pepper, slic't ginger, salt, tyme and some other sweet herbs being finely minced, and two or three blades of mace; stew it the space of two hours and a little before you dish it, take the yolks of six new laid eggs, dissolve them with some grape verjuyce, give it a walm or two on the fire, and serve it up hot.

I served my modern version of this rabbit dish with tagliatelle and found that the creamy sauce blended well with the smooth noodles.

HASHED RABBIT

SERVES 4

1 × 2-lb (1-kg) rabbit, cut into pieces or rabbit portions
1 pint (600 ml) white wine
10 fl oz (300 ml) well-seasoned stock
Bouquet garni including thyme, parsley, marjoram and bay leaf
$\frac{1}{2}$ teaspoon freshly ground black pepper
1-inch (2.5-cm) fresh ginger root, peeled and finely sliced
$\frac{1}{4}$ teaspoon ground mace
3 egg yolks, beaten
Salt
$\frac{1}{4}$ teaspoon wine vinegar

Pre-heat the oven to gas mark 4, 350°F (180°C).

Drop the rabbit pieces into a pan of boiling water, bring back to the boil and boil for 3 minutes. Then lift them out and rinse under a cold tap. Put the rabbit pieces with the wine, stock, bouquet garni, pepper, ginger and mace into a casserole and bring quickly to the boil. Cover and cook in the oven for $1\frac{1}{2}$ hours. When cooked, take out the rabbit pieces and keep them hot on a serving plate. Strain 14 fl oz (400 ml) of the cooking liquor into a small saucepan and mix in the beaten egg yolks. Return the pan to a very low heat and, stirring all the time, heat the sauce until it thickens. Season with salt to taste. Do not let it boil. Add the vinegar in small drops to taste. Spoon the sauce over the rabbit and serve.

Mealtimes during the seventeenth century gradually became later. By the end of Elizabeth I's reign in 1603 breakfasts of cold meats, cheese and ale were eaten between 6 and 7 a.m. Dinner, the main meal of the day, was some time between 11 a.m. and noon while a light supper was taken around 6 p.m. Pepys was already dining after noon and by the 1760s the fashionable in London were dining as late as 7 p.m., although country people continued to keep earlier hours. Breakfast, still a substantial meal of cold meats and ale, was eaten around 9 or 10 a.m. in town and supper had became a late-night snack. Afternoon tea filled the gap between breakfast and dinner with tea and bread and butter or buttered toast.

The serving of meals as well as the cooking became more ordered during the seventeenth century. Dinner plates of pottery or pewter had already replaced medieval trencher breads and forks slowly became more popular, although many people, Louis XIV of France reputedly amongst them, always ate with their fingers. Meals were served in courses with the dishes, both sweet and savoury, laid out on the table in geometric patterns. This manner of serving a meal came to be known as 'French style' and remained in fashion until the middle of the nineteenth century. A typical meal was served in three courses. The first two courses had a main central dish, such as soup or roast, set in the centre of the table, around which four lesser dishes or entrées were arranged. Outside these dishes were the *hors-d'œuvres* – the name at this time referring to their position on the table, not to their place in the menu as nowadays. The third course of fruits and confectionery was laid out in similar patterns.

V e g e t a b l e s   i n   L o n d o n

London in the seventeenth and eighteenth centuries was already the commercial centre of England. The court, government and rich merchants all lived there. It was by far the biggest town in England and drew to it the produce from the surrounding countryside. An insight into the provision of vegetables in the capital comes from a vignette of the wife of Oliver Cromwell published after the Restoration in the satirical *Court and kitchen of Elizabeth Cromwell*: A country woman living on the outskirts of London had some early green peas. Thinking to get a good price for them she carried a peck and a half (about 3 gallons) in a basket up to London. On her way she passed through the Strand where a cook at the Savoy offered her an angel (10 shillings/50 pence) for her peas. She refused and went on to Whitehall where she was directed to Mrs Cromwell's chamber:

An abundance of fresh vegetables and fruit from the garden in An Allegory of Summer *by the late-sixteenth-century painter Lucas van Valkenborch.*

one of her maids came out and understanding it was a present and rarity carried it in to the Protectoress, who out of her princely munificence sent her a crown, [5 shillings/25 pence] which the maid put into her hand. The woman seeing this baseness and the frustration of her hopes, and remembering the cook at the Savoy threw back the money into the maid's hands and desired her to fetch back her peas, for that she was offered five shillings more for them before she brought them thither.

She returned to the Savoy and sold them to the cook. Perhaps he cooked them according to the recipe given in *Le Cuisinier François*, already translated into English two years after publication in France. Peas were 'put into a pan with some butter, and let them cook with a hearted lettuce. When they are well cooked with a bouquet garni and well seasoned, serve them garnished with lettuce.' This is still a popular French recipe today. It requires fresh peas as you cannot use frozen peas successfully for this dish.

PETITS POIS À LA FRANÇAISE

SERVES 4

2 small-hearted lettuces (Little Gem) or hearts of lettuce
1½ oz (40 g) butter
1 lb (450 g) fresh peas, shelled
1 teaspoon sugar
Salt and freshly ground black pepper

Wash the lettuces and cut each heart in half. Melt the butter in a saucepan and put in the peas. Cover the pan and cook over a very gentle heat for 10 minutes. Then tuck the lettuces into the peas and add the sugar and seasoning. Use a fireproof bowl to cover the pan. Choose one which fits tightly so no steam can escape. Pour a cup or two of cold water into the bowl covering the pan to encourage condensation from the cooking to fall back into the pan. Continue cooking on the lowest heat possible for another $1\frac{1}{4}$ hours.

Around the north and western peripheries of London numbers of intensively cultivated small market gardens grew fruit and vegetables for the capital, manured by its night-soil. Their produce was sold throughout London, from barrows or in markets – the biggest and best of these was Covent Garden. The author of a late-eighteenth-century guide to London advised housewives to go there for good fruit and vegetables because although the prices might be higher the quality on the whole was satisfactory. 'Country people,' he wrote, 'would never relish the fruit and vegetables sold in London,' as they were used to really fresh vegetables and fruit.

New Drinks from the East and West

During the seventeenth century the European nations enormously increased their trading activities throughout the world. The English traded with the new colonies in North America, with the West Indies and with the East. By the middle of the century they were importing sugar from plantations in Barbados and Jamaica; they carried slaves from Africa to work the plantations and salt cod from Europe to feed them. In the East they traded between India and China, taking silver to China in return for her silks and tea. The Dutch at the beginning of the century traded grain from eastern Europe, carried wine from Gascony to sell in the Baltic, salt from the Persian Gulf and tea from China. During the century, however, their supremacy in the Far East was overtaken by the English who, by the end of the century, controlled virtually all the tea trade from Canton. One of the results of all this trading activity was the introduction of hot drinks to seventeenth-century Europe. Tea, coffee and chocolate all became popular at this time.

Tea had been drunk and valued in China for over 1000 years before it was first brought to Europe by the Portuguese in the middle of the sixteenth century. By the end of the century the Dutch were bringing very small quantities to France and England. But until the middle of the next century the quantities arriving were not large enough for it to be on general sale. However in 1658 an advertisement in London announced 'that excellent . . . and approved China drink called by the Chineans Tcha' was for sale at the Sultaness Head Coffee-House by the Royal Exchange. Pepys soon tasted his first cup and by 1660 was 'sending for a cup of tee'. The East India Company started importing tea to England in 1669 and by 1700 imported 20 000 pounds of it from China; in the following ten years this figure trebled. The Europeans at this time did not know how tea was grown nor how it was prepared; it was only in the nineteenth century that they finally obtained cuttings and established tea plantations outside China in Java, Ceylon and India.

The first teas to reach Europe were green or unfermented. Green tea has a light astringent flavour due to the absence of any fermentation. The leaves immediately they are picked are rolled and steamed to prevent any fermentation. However, before the end of the seventeenth century bohea, or black tea, had arrived in England. The leaves for black tea are fermented before they are steamed and dried, which gives a stronger less astringent flavour.

At the beginning of the eighteenth century tea was made very weak and drunk with sugar but no milk. During that century tea became popular with all classes of people. The rich bought the delicate, expensive varieties while the poor drank the cheapest tea – often greatly adulterated – and made it very weak with only a few leaves to the pot. Tea became the standard breakfast drink with bread and butter or toast, and was drunk again in the afternoon and also after dinner in the evening. By the middle of the century some people had started to add a little cream or milk to their tea to counteract the acidic effects of the tannin. The diarist Parson Woodforde frequently notes in his diary that he took tea with friends and occasionally he lists his purchases of green and bohea tea. In March 1764 he bought an ounce of green tea for 6 pence and an ounce of bohea for $4\frac{1}{2}$ pence. Thirteen years later the cost of tea had risen and Parson Woodforde had to pay 10 shillings and 6 pence for a pound of tea from Andrew the Smuggler.

In a review of the state of the poor written at the end of the eighteenth century, Sir Frederic Eden notes that 'in poor families, tea is not only the usual beverage in the morning and evening, but it is usually drunk in large quantities at dinner.' By 1800 tea had replaced beer as the normal drink for many English farm labourers and by the 1840s it was among the poverty-line foods in England listed by Engels. In the same way that for centuries a hot drink of tea changed a cold meal into the semblance of a hot meal for Chinese peasants – sometimes in China the drink was only hot water, called 'tea' – so now it did the same for the poor in England, where a meal of bread and cheese or cold bacon was transformed by hot tea.

Coffee was another new drink to be introduced into Europe during the

Above: A popular late seventeenth-century coffee house like the ones often visited by Pepys.

However, coffee-drinking did not meet with universal approval (right).

THE
WOMENS
PETITION
AGAINST
COFFEE
REPRESENTING
TO
PUBLICK CONSIDERATION
THE
Grand INCONVENIENCIES accruing
to their SEX from the Excessive
Use of that Drying, Enfeebling
LIQUOR.
Presented to the Right Honorable the
Keepers of the Liberty of *VENUS*.

By a Well-willer

London, Printed 1674.

seventeenth century. The coffee shrub is native to Ethiopia and by the sixteenth century coffee was known and drunk throughout the Muslim world. The first coffee beans arrived in Venice at the beginning of the seventeenth century and in Paris by 1657. A fashion for Turkish goods and styles encouraged its acceptance and by the 1670s itinerant coffee sellers in Paris were selling cups of coffee with sugar for two sous. Coffee shops or *cafés* opened and became meeting places for all kinds of literary and political figures. So popular did they become as meeting places that Louis XIV inquired whether they should be closed down because 'in several places in Paris where coffee is served, there are assemblies of all sorts of people, and especially foreigners', but the cafés survived. It has been suggested that coffee drinking in France was enormously influential because it provided the first opportunity for people to gather socially without getting drunk.

In England the first coffee shop opened in Oxford in 1650, and was quickly followed by others in London. Pepys frequently visited coffee houses to do business or meet friends. 'At noon I to the Exchange and meeting Shales, he and I to the Coffee-house and talked then of our victualling matters . . .' Many of the early coffee houses became associated with dining clubs patronised by famous political or literary figures. The landlords of the coffee houses set aside rooms for the clubs' use. The Virginia and Baltic coffee house of the eighteenth century was the foundation of the modern Baltic Exchange. Other clubs grew out of chocolate houses, the most famous being White's, although no longer on the site of the original White's chocolate house.

Bars of chocolate as we know them today were not invented until Victorian times, but chocolate to drink has been popular throughout Europe since the seventeenth century. *The Public Advertiser* of 16 June 1657 announced that in Bishopsgate Street in Queens Head Alley 'is an excellent West Indian drink called chocolate to be sold where you may have it readily at any time and also unmade at reasonable rates'.

When Cortes first landed in Mexico in 1519 the Aztec emperor Montezuma personally offered him a dark spicy drink called *xocolatl*. Chocolate in Aztec belief had a divine origin, and it played an essential part in their religious rituals. The Spaniards in Mexico quickly learned to appreciate this comforting though slightly bitter drink. They added sugar, cinnamon and vanilla to it in place of the chillies in the Aztec recipe. When chocolate was first introduced to Spain it was reserved for the court alone. Its recipe was a state secret, and

An early-nineteenth-century French itinerant chocolate seller.

only monasteries renowned for their pharmaceutical abilities were entrusted with its preparation. However, by the middle of the seventeenth century the art of making drinking chocolate had spread throughout Europe. Pepys sampled the new drink shortly after it was advertised and found it pleasing. By 1700 chocolate was a fashionable breakfast beverage throughout Western Europe.

There are a number of recipes from the beginning of the eighteenth century explaining in detail how to prepare drinking chocolate. Some people even went as far as having a special pot which could be put over the fire in which to make their chocolate, while a whisk was considered essential to raise the foam. This recipe from Rebecca Price's collection of recipes published as *The Compleat Cook* is headed 'To make chocolate the Lady Howards way: whch [*sic*] is the best'.

> To a pinte and quarter of water, break or slice in foure ounces of chocolate, set it on the fire, stiring it sometimes, as soon as it boyles take it off ye fire and mill it well, then set it on again and if it will carry a good froath, it is enough, if not, boyle it longer and when it is well boyled sweeten it to your tast with fine suger and then mill it very well poureing 3 or 4 spoonefulls at a time in your cupps and when you have almost filled a cup, scim some of the froath with a spoon off as you mill it and lay it on the top of your cup, and if it begins to be cold before you have filled all your cupp, heat it over the fire again.

Tea and coffee and chocolate marked a revolution in the style of drinks in the West, because until they became customary the only hot drink ever taken was mulled wine. They are all naturally rather bitter in flavour. Each one was taken with sugar, and their popularity accounted in part for the rise in demand for sugar at that time. In previous centuries sugar had been a rich man's luxury, sparingly used. Sugar came to Europe first from the Middle East and then from Spain. The first sugar refinery in Europe was established in Amsterdam in the thirteenth century. By the seventeenth century sugar plantations run by slave labour in the Caribbean and Brazil sent sugar to a Europe where demand was growing rapidly. The English, and particularly their royalty, seem to have had a great affection for sweets as this description of Elizabeth I by a German traveller who met her shows: 'The Queen, in the sixty-fifth year of her age, very majestic; her face oblong, fair but wrinkled; her eyes small, yet black and pleasant; her nose a little hooked, her lips narrow, and her teeth black – a defect the English seem subject to, from their too great use of sugar'. In England the price of sugar dropped from 1 shilling and 6 pence a pound at the beginning of the seventeenth century to 6 pence a pound at its end. The annual consumption of sugar in 1700 was 4 pounds per head; by 1730 it had doubled.

Foods from the New World

The discovery of America introduced Europeans to a number of unfamiliar vegetables. Kidney beans were easily absorbed into European cooking, but maize remained until very recent times an animal food, except in a band of mountainous lands running from the Pyrenees, through northern Italy, where they made polenta, into Romania. Nasturtiums from the West Indies quickly became popular with both gardeners and cooks who used their brightly coloured flowers and piquant leaves in salads and preserved their peppery seeds and buds in vinegar. But of all the foods discovered in the New World probably among those with the greatest impact on European eating habits were potatoes, turkeys and chocolate. Potatoes first came to Europe as part of the food stores for Spanish ships sailing home from South America. From Spain they were introduced to Italy and then probably France. Sir Francis Drake brought them directly to England from the Caribbean in 1586. Within ten years Gerard wrote of the potato in his *Herball* 'It groweth naturally in America where it was first discovered as reported..., since which time I have received rootes here from Virginia, ... which grow and prosper in my garden as in their owne native country'. According to Gerard potatoes were 'either rolled in the embers, or boiled and eaten with oil, vinegar and pepper or dressed any other way by the hand of some cunning in cookerie.' By 1615 they were being cooked in great pies with meats and artichokes, but they remained a curiosity in English cooking for the rest of the century. In mainland Europe they were regarded with great suspicion. Some people even believed that they caused leprosy, and they were held to be fit only for animals, except in times of famine, until the end of the eighteenth century. However, in Ireland by the middle of the seventeenth century they had already become an established peasant staple food. English cookbooks by the 1740s have many ingenious recipes for their use. In *Adam's luxury and Eve's cookery* published in 1744 there are no fewer than twenty different recipes for cooking and serving potatoes.

> Some People when they are boil'd, have a Sauce ready to put over them, made with Butter, Salt, and Pepper; others use Gravy sauces, others Ketchup, and some eat them boiled with only Pepper and Salt; some cut the large ones in slices and fry them with Onions, others stew them with Salt, Pepper, Ale or Water. It is a common way also to boil them first, and then peel them and lay them in the Dipping-pan under roasting Meat. Another way very much used in Wales, is to bake them with Herrings, mixed with layers of Pepper, Vinegar, Salt, sweet Herbs and Water. Also they cut Mutton in Slices and lay them in a Pan and on them Potatoes and Spices and then another Layer of all the same with half a Pint of Water; this they stew, covering all with Cloths round the Stew-pan, and account it excellent...

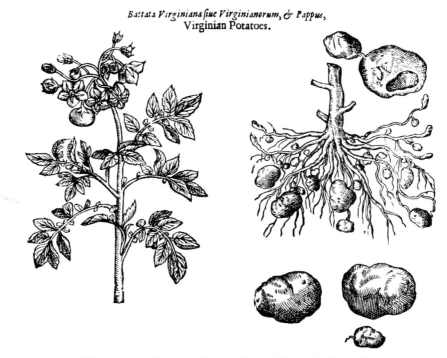

Battata *Virginiana* ſiue *Virginianorum, & Pappus,*
Virginian Potatoes.

The potato—from an illustration in Gerard's Herball.

But there is no mention of fried potatoes or chips as we know them today; they were not to come for another hundred years.

One reason for the slow acceptance of potatoes in Europe must have been that they made a poor flour substitute and a dull garden vegetable. There was little place for them in the contemporary cookery scene. Turkeys were a different matter. Turkeys were brought to Europe from Mexico by the Spaniards somewhere around 1523. The English name 'turkey' probably arose because Levantine merchants, who often called in at Seville on their way from the eastern Mediterranean, first brought them to England around 1524. Certainly by the 1540s turkeys were popular birds for feasts both at the French court and in England. During the next hundred years they gradually replaced swans, peacocks and bustards as festive roasts. They became a relatively cheap and common table bird, roasted, stuffed, baked and in pies; *The English Huswife* gives a recipe for spit-roasting a turkey. By the 1650s Pepys' wife was keeping her own turkeys in London and they were on their way to becoming part of the English Christmas. On 1 January 1659 Pepys notes in his diary that his wife dressed the cold remains of a turkey for their dinner, just as so many people in more recent times have done.

Although chocolate had very quickly become a popular drink, as an ingredient for cooking its adoption was much slower. There are a few late-seventeenth-century recipes for chocolate creams, but these all seem to be derived from chocolate drinks. One of the earliest recipes which used chocolate as an ingredient is *macreuse en ragoût au chocolat* in Massialot's *Le Cuisinier roial et bourgeois* of 1691. *Macreuse* is a kind of wild duck like a widgeon or teal.

Having plucked and cleaned your widgeon, wash it; blanch it in boiling water, and afterwards put it in a pot and season it with salt, pepper, bay leaf and bouquet garni: make a little chocolate and add that. At the same time prepare a ragout [stew] with livers, mushrooms, morels, truffles and a measure of chestnuts. When the widgeon is cooked and served onto the plate pour over the ragout and serve garnished with what you wish.

It is very interesting to compare this recipe with a popular modern Mexican festival recipe which uses chocolate in a similar manner. The origins of this recipe are obscure but it is claimed to have been invented in a convent in Pueblo. It has many features in common with European medieval recipes – such as its use of ground almonds, raisins, a mixture of spices and bread as a

Roasting a turkey in New England in the early nineteenth century: the familiar problems of getting such a large bird properly cooked appear to be of long standing.

thickening agent, but these are combined with four native American ingredients, turkey, chocolate, chillies and tomatoes. The cooking technique, of boiling the meat before it is fried and preparing the sauce ragout separately, is also an indication of its possible early European origins.

TURKEY IN CHILLI AND CHOCOLATE SAUCE

SERVES 6

12 dried red chillies

1 × 5 lb (2.25 kg) turkey

Salt

1 oz (25 g) lard or solid white cooking fat

2 medium-sized onions, chopped

3 cloves of garlic, chopped

$\frac{1}{4}$ teaspoon aniseed

$\frac{1}{4}$ teaspoon ground cloves

$\frac{1}{2}$ teaspoon ground cinnamon

6 tablespoons sesame seeds, toasted

6 oz (175 g) blanched almonds

2 oz (50 g) seedless raisins

12 oz (350 g) tomatoes, blanched, peeled, seeded and chopped

2 slices stale bread or toast, cut into small pieces

$1\frac{1}{2}$ oz (40 g) bitter chocolate

Slit the chillies and remove the seeds. Put the chillies into 15 fl oz (450 ml) warm water and leave to soak for 1 hour. Meanwhile cut the turkey into serving portions and put into a large casserole. Cover with lightly salted water and bring to the boil. Simmer for 1 hour and then lift out the turkey pieces and drain well. Reserve the turkey broth and wash and dry the casserole. Heat the lard or cooking fat in a big frying-pan and brown the turkey pieces, a few at a time, and then return them to the clean casserole.

Mix the chillies and their water with the onions, garlic, aniseed, cloves, cinnamon, 4 tablespoons sesame seeds, almonds, raisins, tomatoes and bread. Using a food processor work the mixture a little at a time into a very coarse heavy paste. Take care not to over work. Fry this paste in the lard left from frying the turkey for about 5 minutes, stirring all the time. Break the chocolate into small pieces and add it to the mixture together with 15 fl oz (450 ml) of the reserved turkey broth. Continue stirring until the chocolate has melted and then pour the sauce over the turkey. Cover the casserole and simmer gently for another 30 minutes. Check the seasoning and serve sprinkled with the remaining toasted sesame seeds.

The diet of North American settlers

The first English settlers in Virginia were faced with finding foods for themselves in an unknown land. They brought with them a few farm animals such as cows, sheep and pigs, and some seeds, but in general were dependent on local foods and plants. The first summer before the harvest was a time of great shortage and many of the first settlers died of starvation and sickness before any supply ships arrived. Of necessity they had to learn from the native Indians. Letters tell of failures of the traditional English crops of wheat, barley and oats, and their dependence on Indian corn. Indian corn or maize was the principal American Indian grain and the settlers learnt how to cultivate and cook it from the Indians.

An account of the lives of some French settlers and their Indian neighbours in Illinois written by Lamothe Cadillac in the 1690s describes how the maize was crushed with a heavy wooden pestle in a hollowed out tree trunk and then winnowed and sieved. The maize meal was boiled into a gruel with water and cooked fish was stirred in before it was eaten. Cadillac adds that this was not a dainty food, but sustaining. Bread made of maize meal was baked under hot ashes or in hot sand – this he said was good when you are hungry. The French also dried pumpkins, another native American vegetable, and cooked them with corn and meat.

The diet of the pioneers who first settled in Western Pennsylvania during the eighteenth century was also simple and coarse. The forest provided for much of their needs; game, fish and berries in abundance. Indian corn was their most valuable food. For breakfast at harvest time they ate boiled or roasted corn on the cob; the standard supper throughout the year was mush of corn meal boiled in milk or water and molasses – a sweet syrup separated out from sugar crystals during sugar refining and much cheaper than refined sugar. Much of their cooking was done outside because the first log cabins had no chimneys. They used rendered bear and opossum fat for frying. Leavened bread was a rare commodity, although many families baked a corn meal bread called johny cake in the embers of the fire. A recipe for johny cake appears in Amelia Simmons' *American Cookery*, first published in 1796.

Scald 1 pint of milk and put to 3 pints of indian meal, and half pint of flower – bake before the fire. Or scald with milk two thirds of the indian meal, or wet two thirds with boiling water, add salt, molasses and shortening, work up with cold water pretty stiff, and bake as above.

A hundred years later Fanny Farmer in her *Boston Cookery School Cookbook* gave this version of the early settlers' corn meal bread:

GOLDEN CORN CAKE

$\frac{3}{4}$ *cup corn meal*
$1\frac{1}{4}$ *cups flour*
$\frac{1}{4}$ *cup sugar*
4 teaspoons baking powder
$\frac{1}{2}$ *teaspoon salt*
1 cup milk
1 egg
1 tablespoon melted butter

Mix and sift dry ingredients; add milk, egg well-beaten and butter: bake in shallow buttered pan in hot oven twenty minutes.

A modern version uses equal quantities of corn meal and flour – one cup of each – 3 teaspoons of baking powder, and melted shortening or bacon fat in place of the butter. It is baked at gas mark 7, 425°F (220°C).

In Virginia early English settlers learned to cook dried beans with dried corn as a winter dish. By the early nineteenth century it was no longer only a winter dish, as Elizabeth Labbe Cole's manuscript recipe shows: 'for a change I cook these together, cutting Corn from the Cob and cooking with the Beans until tender and about dry. Season with Butter, Cream and Pepper, Salt being added when they are put on to boil.'

New World foods in China

The new food crops discovered in America not only travelled to Europe but to India, the Far East and in particular to China. Sweet potatoes, peanuts, maize and chillies are all native to South America, and all became important foods in China. Sweet potatoes first arrived in China late in the sixteenth century. They were an immediate success because of their high yields, tolerance of poor soils and adverse weather conditions, and also probably because their sweet flavour appealed to a community in which sugar and sweetening were expensive luxuries. During the eighteenth and nineteenth centuries the Chinese population increased in the order of 300 per cent. There were too many mouths and, even in China, too little room to grow the food to put in them. Sweet potatoes became a staple food for many peasants and by 1800 they made up almost 50 per cent of the annual food intake of northern Chinese peasants.

A thirteenth-century recipe for yams – a native Chinese vegetable – in which they were cooked and then sliced and soaked in honey, was rewritten in the nineteenth century using sweet potatoes instead of yams. It was a luxury dish, just as it had been in the thirteenth century.

Piper Indicum medium.

The new arrival – chilli pepper from a herbal published in 1613.

BRAISED SWEET POTATOES WITH HONEY

SERVES 6–8

---

1 lb (450 g) purple-skinned sweet potatoes

---

5 oz (150 g) Chinese crystal sugar (bought from a Chinese grocer's)

---

7 fl oz (200 ml) water

1½ tablespoons good flower-flavoured honey

Peel and cut the sweet potatoes into big wedge-shaped pieces. Dissolve the sugar in the water in a large thick-bottomed pan, then add the potatoes and honey. Bring just to the boil and simmer very gently for 30 minutes with the pan covered. Afterwards remove the lid and continue simmering until the potatoes are completely soft – about 30 to 40 minutes. Towards the end of the cooking time, if the syrup is much reduced, take care that the potatoes do not burn. Lift them carefully onto a serving dish and spoon the remaining syrup over them. Chill before serving.

Chinese cuisine has always accepted new ingredients from foreign countries and incorporated them into its own established cooking styles. The American foods were no exception. Chillies probably first arrived in China around 1600 although they were not mentioned in print until almost the end of the century. Sichuan and Yunnan cooking, now famous for their generous use of chillies, must have been totally transformed. Maize had arrived earlier. It was first mentioned in print about 1550 but, unlike chillies, it was never a popular crop. The Chinese always preferred rice or wheat-flour noodles to maize foods; as late as the 1970s there was celebration in northern Yunnan 'when yellow [maize] gave way to white [rice]' – when they were able to grow sufficient rice to take the place of maize.

The East in Britain

The British were fascinated by the East throughout the eighteenth century. The East India Company controlled the economy in Bengal and Bihar states, manipulating them for its own interests, and ran its own army virtually independent of the British crown. Vast fortunes were made by those who survived the rigours of the Indian climate. The Company also held a virtual monopoly on the trade with Amoy and Canton in China.

This new interest in the East was reflected in British clothes, furniture and food fashions during the eighteenth century. The British developed a taste for spicy sauces and dishes. Baron Sandys 'picked up in India' the recipe for Worcestershire sauce he gave to Mr Lea (of Lea and Perrins). Hannah Glasse in her *Art of Cooking made plain and easy* (1747) gives a recipe 'to make a curry the Indian way' in which she stews two chickens with onions, thirty peppercorns, a large spoonful of rice and ground coriander seeds until it is cooked, and then puts in 'a Piece of fresh Butter, about as big as a large walnut'. This is a very rudimentary curry compared to modern recipes. Hannah Glasse also has a recipe for making a pellow (*sic* – pilau) the Indian way in which she warns 'to take great Care the rice don't burn to the Pot'. Curry powder did not arrive in Britain until about forty years after Hannah Glasse wrote her book.

The first recipes for mulligatawny (from the Tamil for 'pepper water') soup using curry powder were published at the beginning of the nineteenth century; by the middle of the century it had become an accepted British dish. Mrs Dalgairns gives four mulligatawny soups in her *Practice of cookery*, published in Edinburgh in 1829. Three of her soups are thickened with barley, bread or split peas; however, the fourth, which is given below, is unthickened and is perhaps the closest to a modern mulligatawny soup. There seems no need to enlarge upon Mrs Dalgairns' recipe, although the quantities (for 8) are rather large for modern use.

MULLIGATAWNY OR CURRIE BROTH

Make about two quarts of strong veal broth, seasoned with two onions, a bunch of parsley, salt and pepper; strain it and have ready a chicken, cut into joints and skinned; put it into the broth, with a tablespoon of curry powder; boil the chicken till quite tender, and a little before serving add the juice of a lemon, and stir in a teacupful of cream. Serve boiled rice to eat with this broth.

The British in India

The British community living in India in the eighteenth and nineteenth centuries brought with them British food habits which they adapted to Indian ingredients. Their cooks were Indian and the meals they ate were often a combination of Indian and British dishes, accompanied by European wines. A letter from Calcutta in the 1770s lists the dishes for a family dinner: soup, a roast fowl, rice and curry, mutton pie, a fore-quarter of lamb, rice pudding, tarts, very good cheese and excellent Madeira.

Eighty years later an anonymous cookbook published in Calcutta sounds the unmistakable voice of the nineteenth-century British middle class when it advised the reader 'In many families the remains of cold meat, if not required for other purposes, are made into curry: cold roast or boiled mutton is admirably adapted for the purpose; and in ninety-nine cases out of a hundred consumers cannot tell the difference.'

Various British cookbooks were published in India to help colonial house-wives struggling with unfamiliar foods and seasons. They gave a wide selection of recipes – one included roast antelope among the more familiar beef and chicken and suggested using bustard in place of turkey. There were also many curry and chutney recipes using foods from the local markets. An anonymous recipe book published in Bombay in 1852 used Western ingredients for some Indian dishes. 'Tomata or love apple' chutney appeared among other chutneys made with tamarinds, mangoes, limes, plantains, and aubergines – a vegetable unknown in Britain at that time, although well known in southern Europe.

A mid-nineteenth-century colonial housewife in India supervising her servants.

Indian chutneys and pickles became very popular with the British and have remained so. In the margin by the side of the following recipe from the 1852 book a nineteenth-century hand has written 'very nice'.

RIPE TOMATA OR LOVE APPLE CHUTNEY

Take one or more large ripe tomatas; strip off the skin; then divide and remove the seeds and juice; to the pulp that remains add a little salt, as much chopped onions, cut very fine, as is equal to about one half the tomata pulp, a tablespoon of vinegar, a little celery cut very fine, and one or more green chillis, according to taste; if you desire to make this chutney into a salad [dressing], add a tablespoon of thick cream.

5

FOOD *and* MACHINES *in the* WEST – *from* 1750 *to* 1900

Parson Woodforde's England

One of the best accounts of eighteenth-century country life can be found in the diaries kept by Parson Woodforde. For nearly fifty years he recorded in great detail the comfortable rural life in Norfolk which he and his gentry neighbours enjoyed. His diaries are full of the fresh foods of the countryside and descriptions of the meals they ate. These illustrate the rural and seasonal nature of their lives through the years. The parson fished and hunted enthusiastically and the results of his sport were served at the dinner table. Hares were coursed and appeared the next day for dinner, apparently without being hung; 'a brace of the best trout' were sent as a gift to a neighbour. Meats of all kinds appear in the diaries; mutton with capers was a favourite dish and each Christmas Day six or seven poor old men of the parish were given a dinner of roast sirloin of beef and plum pudding. Most weeks fresh fish was fetched from Norwich; cod's head with oyster sauce was a favourite, but mackerel, lobster, sole, skate and whiting all appeared on the parsonage table.

They had fresh vegetables from the parsonage garden. Bowls of fresh strawberries and raspberries were served for dessert in June; peaches, nectarines, plums and pears in September. Plum pudding, syllabubs – apparently sometimes rather indifferent – and fruit tarts of every variety were made at home. The parson himself supervised the home-brewing of beer, and bought gin and brandy from local smugglers.

In April 1787 fresh skate was fetched from Norwich, and a neighbour sent 'some fine bunches of asparagus and 2 cucumbers, both very great rarities at

An eighteenth-century gentleman surveying his walled kitchen garden.

this time [of year].' The following day for a dinner with friends there was skate with oyster sauce, knuckle of veal, a tongue, a fine forequarter of lamb and plum pudding with a second course of asparagus, lobster, raspberry tarts (were these perhaps made with preserved raspberries?), and black caps (baked apples) in custard, and also radishes and the cucumbers.

The parson's niece was 'very busy all the morning' at the end of January 1782 'making Cakes, Tarts, Custards, and Jellies for to Morrow'. On the following day the local squire and his family 'dined, spent the afternoon, and stayed with us until after 8 o'clock this evening. I gave them for Dinner a Leg of Mutton boiled and Capers, a boiled Fowl and a Tongue, a batter Pudding, a fine Turkey rosted, Fryed Rabbit, Tarts, Custards and Jellies. – Almonds and Raisins, Oranges and Apples after. Port wine, Mountain, Porter and Ale.'

In June the following year dinner at the parsonage was full of garden

Eighteenth-century tea-time, with bread and butter at the side, painted by Richard Collins.

produce 'a leg of Lamb boiled, Carrotts and Turnips, a Rump of Beef rosted and Cucumbers, a fine Ham, Peas and Beans, four Chicken rosted, Gooseberry Tarts and Custards – Desert – Some very fine Oranges, Almonds and Raisins and plenty of Strawberries and Cream – all which looked very well.'

How were these dishes cooked? The parson disliked the French style of dressing foods with sauces and condemned one meal as 'spoilt by being so frenchified in dressing'. British taste was for plain cooking, leaving foods to taste of themselves, in direct opposition to French *haute cuisine* in which the additions the cook made to foods and their flavour were essential to the enjoyment of the dish. In the parson's diaries can be found the flowering of the British style of cooking which first appeared in late-Elizabethan country houses two centuries earlier. It was a style of cooking based ideally on plenty of good country produce locally available and cooked by people with an understanding of the countryside and its seasons. The British expected to eat good meat in large quantities – joints of beef weighing between 30 and 40 pounds were served at the Duke of Grafton's table – and of a quality that needed no sauce. Such a style of cuisine had no social, only economic, limitations.

Many British authors of cookery books at the time were women who were not themselves professional cooks, and wrote as much for the mistresses of country houses as for their cooks. Hannah Glasse was the most successful in this genre – it is conceivable that the parsonage might even have had a copy of her book. *The Art of Cooking made plain and easy* was published in 1747, and reprinted many times in the following fifty years. Hannah Glasse wrote a passionate indictment against the extravagances of French cuisine and proclaimed herself to be an economical cook, although to our modern eyes, recipes such as her pancake batter made with 1 pint of cream, 8 eggs, and $\frac{1}{2}$lb of melted butter mixed with flour to make a thin batter, appear extravagant as well as unhealthy. But for her well-off country readers at that time, cream, butter and eggs were virtually always to hand. Butcher's meat had to be brought from the nearest town, involving a journey possibly of some length, so it was only fetched at intervals. Butcher's meat was meat that required specialised killing and cutting, unlike rabbits and chickens which were done at home. Curiously, killing a pig was also considered a domestic affair although it was often performed by a visiting butcher. Hannah advises 'If you live in the Country where you cannot always have Gravy Meat, when your Meat comes from the Butcher take a piece of Beef, a piece of Veal and a piece of

Mutton ... and a very little piece of Bacon ...' and make a stock ready for when it is needed. Perhaps one of the most typical of her British-style recipes is that for jugged hare, where the fresh country ingredients are left to speak for themselves:

> Cut it into little Pieces, lard here and there with little Slips of Bacon, season them with a very little Pepper and Salt, and put them into an earthen Jugg with a blade or two of Mace, an Onion stuck with Cloves and a Bundle of Sweet Herbs; cover the Jugg or Jar you do it in, so close that nothing can get in; then set it in a Pot of boiling Water, keep the Water boiling, and three Hours will do it; then turn it onto a Dish and take out the Onion and Sweet Herbs and send it to the Table hot.

I followed Mrs Glasse's recipe but used a casserole instead of the jug and I changed the traditional cooking style to cooking in an oven because of the possible danger that some pieces of hare might not be cooked at a sufficiently high temperature if the only source of heat was boiling water.

JUGGED HARE

SERVES 4

2 lb (1 kg) saddle and back legs of fresh hare, not frozen
1 rasher fat bacon
$\frac{1}{4}$ teaspoon ground mace
1 medium onion, stuck with 3 cloves
Bouquet garni of thyme, parsley and marjoram
$\frac{1}{4}$ teaspoon freshly ground black pepper
Salt

Pre-heat the oven to gas mark 3, 325°F (160°C).

Initially follow the method exactly as Mrs Glasse's recipe above except for the use of the casserole instead of the jug. Seal the casserole with tin foil under the cover and place it in a roasting tin. Fill the roasting tin with hot water to half-way up the casserole and cover it completely with more tin foil. Place in the oven and cook for 3 hours. Add more boiling water to the roasting tin when necessary. Before serving remove the onion and bouquet garni and check the seasoning.

The unselfconscious abundance of food seen in Parson Woodforde's diaries was noticeably lacking in the diets of agricultural workers in the same phase of time. During the eighteenth century the price of food, particularly wheat, rose steeply. Towards the end of the century potatoes became increasingly popular as a staple for the poor; they were easy to cook and when cooked provided the semblance of a hot meal. On the whole, north countrymen ate better than southern; they had oatmeal and potatoes and were not dependent on wheat for their basic staple, and so were protected to an extent from the steep rises in wheat prices. Rural workers in the south with little or no space for gardens could not grow potatoes and other vegetables, and lived almost exclusively on bread with a little salt bacon or cheese. If they were lucky they might have meat once a week, but they were always short of fuel for cooking. Few of them could afford beer and instead drank tea with every meal.

Even at the end of the nineteenth century the foods eaten in the rural south by agricultural workers had not changed markedly from those described in accounts of southern country life a hundred years earlier. Flora Thompson's idealised account of her childhood in the rural Oxfordshire of the 1880s in *Lark Rise to Candleford* speaks of bacon from the family pig, kept in a sty at the back of each cottage, eaten with fresh vegetables all in their season from the cottage gardens together with bread, bought from the baker, and home-made lard flavoured with rosemary. Flour for the daily pudding was milled from the family's gleanings in the fields after the harvest.

Fresh meat was a luxury only seen in a few of the cottages on Sunday, when six-pennyworth of pieces would be bought to make a meat pudding. If a small joint came their way as a Saturday night bargain, those without oven grates would roast it by suspending it on a string before the fire, with one of the children in attendance as turnspit. Or a 'pot-roast' would be made by placing the meat with a little lard or other fat in an iron saucepan and keeping it well shaken over the fire. But, after all, as they said, there was nothing to beat a 'toad'. For this the meat was enclosed whole in a suet crust and well boiled, a method which preserved all the delicious juices of the meat and provided a good pudding into the bargain.

The *Old Statistical Account of Scotland* compiled at the end of the eighteenth century also gives perhaps an over optimistic view of the state of farm workers in the parish of Strachu and Stralachan in the poor county of Argyle where

> there are few parts of the kingdom where this class of men has more reason to be contented with their situation. There being no market contiguous, they lay in for their winter provision the half of a small cow or bullock, weighing from 10 to 12 stone tron weight, or a proportionable quantity of mutton, and a store of herring. This with potatoes is their food for half a year. For the other half they live on oat-meal, milk and sometimes fresh herrings. The potatoes, indeed generally last three quarters of the year. Such of them as have a milk cow, which most of them have, gather as much dung as enables them to raise a sufficient quantity of this useful root. The farmers always give them as much land as they can furnish manure for.

The parishioners of Stradu and Stralachan were particularly fortunate because their parish was close enough to the sea for them to buy fresh herrings. The generally better diet for rural workers in Scotland compared with those in England resulted in army recruits with far finer physiques coming from Scotland than from England in the first half of the nineteenth century.

Restaurants – the beginnings

For centuries, inns in England and France had provided food as well as shelter for travellers, but the quality of the food offered was often poor with little or no choice. It is perhaps significant that that indefatigable recorder of meals, Parson Woodforde, never detailed a meal eaten at an inn on his various travels – on one visit to London he briefly mentions he dined on 'beef à la mode' at a tavern. For another traveller at the end of the eighteenth century the York Inn in Dover had undrinkable wine, musty fowls and stinking partridges, all charged at an exorbitant rate. Dr Johnson described the roast mutton served at an inn as 'ill-fed, ill-killed, ill-kept, and ill-drest'. However, some travellers fared better. The landlord of the Jolly Sandboys in Dickens'

The Old Curiosity Shop prepared a stew of tripe, cowheel, bacon and steak together with beans, cauliflowers, new potatoes and asparagus 'all working up together in one delicious gravy'. Richard Briggs who was cook at the Globe Tavern, Fleet Street in the 1780s, in his book *The Art of cookery* gives a recipe for a similar rich and nourishing stew which might well have met with Mr Codlin's approval. He called it 'a West-Indian pepper-pot' because of the cayenne pepper in the recipe. 'Pepper-pot' was a popular recipe at the end of the eighteenth century and appears in different forms in several cookery books of the time.

> Take two pounds of lean Veal, the same of Mutton cut them small, with a pound of lean Ham, put them in a stew pan and about 4 lbs of Brisket of Beef cut in square pieces, with six Onions, two Carrots, four heads of Celery, four Leeks, two Turnips, well washed, a bundle of Sweet Herbs, some All Spice, Cloves and Mace and half a pint of Water; sweat them well for half an Hour and then pour four pints of boiling Water into it, and skim it well, boil it gently for three Hours, then strain it off, take out the Pieces of Beef; then put a quarter pound of Butter in the Stew Pan, and melt it; put two Spoons of Flour and stir it about until it is smooth, then by degrees pour in your Soup and stir it about to keep from lumping; put the Pieces of Beef in; have ready two Carrots cut into quarters, four Turnips in quarters boiled until tender, take the Spawn of a Lobster, bruise it fine and put it in to colour it with a dozen Heads of Greens boiled tender; make some Flour and Water into a Paste and make it into Balls as big as a Walnut, boil them well in Water, and put them in. Boil it up gently for 15 minutes and season it very hot with Cayenne Pepper and Salt, and put it in a Soup Dish and send it in very hot, garnished with sprigs of Cauliflower or Carrots or what you wish.

This kind of dish is a continuing tradition in British domestic cookery and recipes for boiled brisket can be found in modern cookbooks. When I made a more modest version of the pepper-pot using tomato in place of the lobster coral I found it was richer and had a fuller, fresher flavour than most modern stews, although time consuming and expensive to prepare. I changed the traditional brisket to shin beef because it has less fat. For the dumplings I preferred a modern recipe using suet but I have also given Mrs Beeton's traditional version after the recipe. It is possible to prepare part of the pepper-pot the day before you wish to eat it. Cook the meat and vegetable stew the day before and then lift out the beef and strain the stock. Return the shin to the strained stock and leave in the refrigerator overnight. The next day prepare the second lot of vegetables and dumplings and finish the dish as directed.

A WEST INDIAN PEPPER-POT

SERVES 6 OR 8

Half a boiling fowl
4 oz (100 g) lean ham
2½-lb (1.25-kg) piece of shin of beef
1 medium-sized onion
4 carrots
3 white turnips
6 sticks celery
2 leeks
Big bouquet garni
3 allspice
2 cloves
¼ teaspoon ground mace
8 florets of cauliflower
1 head of spring greens
1 ripe tomato
1 oz (25 g) butter
3 tablespoons plain flour
¼ teaspoon cayenne pepper
Salt

Suet dumplings

---

4 oz (100 g) self-raising flour

---

2 oz (50 g) suet

$\frac{1}{4}$ teaspoon salt

Freshly ground black pepper

3–4 tablespoons cold water

Chop the boiling fowl into pieces. Cut the ham into cubes and trim and cut the beef into 8 equal portions. Chop the onion, wash, scrape and slice 1 carrot and 1 turnip. Trim, clean and slice all the celery and leeks. Put the vegetables into a large heavy pan with 5 fl oz (150 ml) water, cover and sweat over a low heat until the vegetables are soft. Then add all the meats, including the boiling fowl, and continue cooking, uncovered, until they are all sealed. Slip in the bouquet garni and spices and pour in 2 pints (1.2 litres) of boiling water and bring to the boil. Turn down the heat, skim off the rising scum carefully, cover and leave to simmer for 3 hours.

Meanwhile make your dumplings. Mix the flour with the suet, salt and pepper. Add the water and knead into a smooth soft paste. It should not be sticky. Shape into 8 balls and simmer for 20 minutes in a pan of boiling water. When cooked, drain the dumplings and keep them on one side. Prepare and parboil the remaining carrots, turnips and cauliflower and wash and coarsely shred the spring greens. Skin and de-seed the tomato and finely chop the flesh.

When the stew is ready, lift out the beef and keep on one side. Strain the stock carefully and discard the fowl, ham and vegetables from it. In a clean casserole melt the butter and make a roux with the flour. A little at a time, pour in 2 pints (1.2 litres) of the reserved stock, stirring to prevent it going into lumps, and bring to the boil. Return the beef to the pan and add the cooked dumplings, carrots, turnip and shredded greens. Boil until the greens are just cooked, then add the tomato and season with cayenne pepper and salt to taste. Garnish with the cauliflower and serve hot.

In a recipe for flour and water dumplings Mrs Beeton uses 8 oz (225 g) flour, 5 fl oz (150 ml) of water and a pinch of salt. She says 'mix the flour and water together to a smooth paste, previously adding a small quantity of salt. Form this into small round dumplings: drop them into boiling water and boil from $\frac{1}{2}$ to $\frac{3}{4}$ hour.'

In the eighteenth century taverns were the forerunners of restaurants in Britain but lacked the elegance and style which later came to be associated with restaurants. Unlike inns they did not provide lodgings and, on the whole, served men only. Dr Johnson said of them 'There is no private house in which people can enjoy themselves so well as at a capital tavern ... at a tavern, there is a general freedom from anxiety. You are sure of a welcome; and the more noise you make, the more trouble you give, the more good things you call for, the welcomer you are ...' At the same time coffee houses also took to serving fixed priced, fixed menu 'ordinary' meals almost to the exclusion of coffee, and many were virtually indistinguishable from taverns.

Lower down the social scale there were cook-shops selling cooked dishes where working men in London tended to eat their main dinner. Tobias Smollett describes such a place in *The Adventures of Roderick Random* where the narrator found himself 'in the middle of a cook's shop, almost suffocated with the steams of boiled beef, and surrounded by a company consisting chiefly of hackney coachmen, chairmen, draymen, and a few footmen ... who sat eating shin of beef, tripe, cowheel or sausages at separate boards, covered with cloths that turned my stomach.'

In France, unlike Britain, cafés never developed into eating houses and the tavern life extolled by Dr Johnson did not exist. However, there were inns even in the centre of Paris where travellers or working men could obtain meals. The quality of their food appears open to question – as this entry from a Parisian's diary of August 1727 demonstrates: 'Four gentlemen ate salted cod for their dinner at a low class inn in the rue de la Huchette' – a street where today there are still many restaurants – 'immediately they fainted and were carried to the Charité [hospital]; one died two hours later and the others are very ill.' Investigation showed that the salted cod had been washed in lime and alum as well as other drugs to bleach it. A police order prohibiting the bleaching of salted cod was issued and it was suggested that people should eat yellow, salted cod.

The strong hold by the guild of cooked-food merchants in Paris over all the cooked dishes sold in the city inhibited the opening of taverns and eating houses of any quality until the 1760s when a famous court case broke their monopoly. This monopoly had never included the right to sell hot soups. One soup seller named Boulanger, trying to extend his business by selling sheep's feet in white sauce, was taken to court by the guild which claimed that such a dish was a *ragoût* (stew) and therefore within their monopoly. However, Boulanger won the court case and the law was changed to rule that sheep's feet in a white sauce were not a *ragoût* and thus outside the guild's control. Ten years later the first restaurants were making tentative beginnings in Paris, but it took the social upheaval of the Revolution in 1789 to push them into the prominence which they have held since that time. The Revolution transformed the professional opportunities of chefs. Great houses where, before the Revolution, the best food in Paris was found, were closed and at the same time guilds and trade limitations were abolished. The revolutionary political movements brought new clients from the provinces to Paris who needed somewhere to eat and to entertain. Leading chefs who had lost their former aristocratic employers opened 'public tables' or restaurants to meet this demand. In 1789 there were fifty restaurants or 'public tables' in Paris, but by 1800 there were 500.

A French hotel restaurant in the mid-nineteenth century.

The educated gourmet

The development of restaurants in post-Revolutionary France was fundamentally different from the British experience. In France the new bourgeois not only inherited the tastes and style of the old aristocracy but also an interest in the dishes and food available to them. The envy and exclusiveness associated with the old courtly cuisine now encouraged the new rich to go and eat something better than they could afford to provide at home. At the Trois Frères, one of Paris' most famous restaurants in the early nineteenth century, the menu offered a choice of 12 soups, 24 side dishes, 15 to 20 entrées of beef, 20 entrées of mutton, 30 of game or fowl, 16 to 20 of veal, 12 of pastry, 24 of fish, 15 roasts, 50 entremets and 50 entrées of dessert. But shortages imposed by the changing economic climate and the fashion for restraint encouraged cooks to analyse and discipline their cooking. New outstanding chefs, adjusting their work towards public rather than private dining, rapidly refined French cooking. Their new clientele read the writings of such gourmet authors as Grimod and Brillat-Savarin and gained an appreciation and knowledge of the dishes they ate. But, unlike the aristocrats before them, the new bourgeois retained their country roots and an understanding of the origins of their food.

The busy activities in a French pastryshop's kitchen in about 1770.

One of the greatest French chefs of all times was Carême, who worked for such patrons as the Prince Regent, Czar Alexander and the Rothschilds. By the 1820s, when French society was recovering from the turbulence of the Revolution and the monarchy had been restored, Carême's dedication to the skills of his profession had become a culinary model for nineteenth-century French chefs. In his *L'art de la cuisine française au dix-neuvième siècle* he analysed and systematised the emerging *grande cuisine*. Trained originally as a pastrycook he excelled in contrived decorative centrepieces for the grand dinners which he made fashionable. He extended his skill to the whole field of cookery and his elaborate recipes included precise cooking instructions for the preparation of purées, essences, sauces and garnishes. He aimed at a perfect balance between a few well-chosen flavours, for 'flavours and aromas must be judged not in isolation, but in their mutual relation'. An example of his style of recipe is this one for *Grosse truite saumonée à la Polonaise* (Salmon trout in the Polish manner).

> Clean the fish as usual; then score it five times on each side; fill the cavity with a stuffing made from pike; tie up the head with care; and then roll the fish in a mixture of olive oil, salt, pepper, grated nutmeg, the flesh of two lemons finely minced, two onions cut into slices, parsley, and a few bay leaves and branches of thyme; from time to time turn the fish in the marinade, so that it is all equally seasoned. One hour before it is to be served, lift out the trout, sprinkle with more olive oil and a little white salt, and place it on a big grill which you have previously wiped with oil; then put the grill over a moderate fire, which must be bigger than the grill, in order to concentrate the heat under the trout; each quarter of an hour you should add a few hot coals; and turn the fish after 20 to 25 minutes; then you start again taking care to put the hottest coals under the back of the fish, which needs the most cooking; after it is cooked place the fish on a serving dish with its best side up, and garnish it with a ragout of oysters, prawn tails and mushrooms in a Champagne sauce.

The professionalism of French cooking led to its almost total dominance of all high society food in Europe. By the second half of the nineteenth century it had supplanted the old country house style in fashionable English taste. Cooking and meals equal to the very best could be found in the exclusive clubs of central London but generally throughout Britain cooking standards were falling. The British showed no general interest in gastronomy. It has been said that the habit of restricting children in Britain to the nursery and nursery fare until their palates had been mortified and then sending them off to boarding schools, in contrast to French children who ate with their parents, was responsible for the abysmal standards of British food. In France diners even at cheaper restaurants had learnt to expect a style of cooking which followed fairly closely the basic tenets of *haute cuisine*, but in Britain there was no such interested or informed clientele. Restaurants had little incentive to develop or maintain such a style of cooking while equally the middle classes had no reason to acquire a habit and taste for eating out. The urban British middle classes by the mid-nineteenth century had lost contact with their own country origins and that of their foods, unlike the French bourgeois who had retained them.

Plain living and high thinking

Under the new industrial conditions in Britain in the first half of the nineteenth century, workers crowded into the growing towns to man the new machines and steam-powered mills, and to mine the coal. In this phase the population of Manchester grew from 75 000 to 400 000. With the growth of these towns a virtually new social class arose. Although numerically small, the urban middle class of 1850, with its large families and armies of servants, accounted for a much greater proportion of total food consumption than its numbers would suggest. Some of the new middle class were rich, while others had incomes little bigger than factory workers, but they all had a margin of income over expenditure and were to have a lasting effect on patterns of food consumption. Their wealth was based on manufacturing and servicing the new cities; they seldom had any knowledge of or connection with the countryside.

The new middle-class housewife, unlike her predecessor in the country houses of the eighteenth century, had nothing to do with the kitchens, and indeed could 'hardly find the way to the kitchen stairs'. By employing numerous domestic servants she was relieved of unladylike drudgery. In most families the cooking was left to working women who were themselves often town bred and had little feeling for or knowledge of the foods they cooked. The middle classes inherited the prejudices of the previous century but lacked the taste and discernment to realise how debased their food had become. Alexis

An artist's impression of a middle-class kitchen in 1846. It would also have had a fire,
a big table and a sink in the scullery.

Soyer, chef at the Reform Club and a leader in the movement towards the
adoption of French cuisine by fashionable British society, complained of the
British custom of 'plunging expensive meats into an ocean of boiling water,
which is thrown away, after having absorbed a great portion of the succulence
of the meat'. He asks why they cannot 'make use of the broth, by diminishing
the quantity of water and simmering them instead of galloping them at a
special railway train speed?' In *The Modern Housewife* he suggests that:

> were the middle classes only but slightly acquainted with the domestic
> cookery of France, they would certainly live better and less expensively
> than at present: very often four or five different little made dishes may be
> made from the remains of a large Sunday's joint, instead of its appearing
> on the table of wealthy tradesmen for several days cold, and often
> unsightly, and backed by a bottle of variegated-coloured pickles ... and
> balanced by a steaming dish of potatoes ... this may be excusable once
> or twice, on a hot summer's day, with an inviting salad, seasoned with
> merely salt, pepper, oil and vinegar, but the continual repetition of that
> way of living in winter is, I consider, a domestic crime.

Such 'crimes', however, were committed far into the twentieth century.

It seems that some of Alexis Soyer's strictures were observed, for Mrs Beeton in her *Book of Household Management* published ten years later gives a number of recipes using cold cooked meats. These 'cold meat cookery' dishes often appear as entrées in her suggested dinner menus. Mrs Beeton, who is perhaps the best known of all cookery book authors, codified and set the seal on British middle-class cooking in the mid-nineteenth century, although she

THE BRITISH DOMESTIC.

"Don't want no Cookery Books, *I* don't. I could tell yer all wot's in 'em on my ead."

"Don't yewshewerly bile ribs o' beef in a fryin'-pan, don't yer?
P'r'aps yer 'll teach yer granmother."

"Never see sich a dirty muck as things make yer hin!
My fault, is it? Oh, yus!"

Struggles with the cook, from Fun, *1878.*

was not herself in any way innovative. Writing at a time when the cost of food was falling and the advantages of the new transport were becoming felt, her writings reinforced the strongly held middle-class belief in thrift and respectability. Plain living, particularly for children, was considered morally healthy. The first edition of her cookery book is filled with economical notes, as in the note that accompanied this recipe.

Cock-a-leekie Soup

Ingredients. – A capon or large fowl (sometimes an old cock, from which the recipe takes its name, is used) which should be trussed as for boiling; 2 or 3 bunches of fine leeks, 5 quarts of stock, pepper and salt to taste.

Mode. – Well wash the leeks (and, if old, scald them in boiling water for a few minutes), taking off the roots and part of the heads, and cut them into lengths of about an inch. Put the fowl into the stock with, at first, one half of the leeks, and allow it to simmer gently. In half an hour add the remaining leeks, and then it may simmer for 3 to 4 hours longer. It should be carefully skimmed, and can be seasoned to taste. In serving take out the fowl and carve it neatly, placing the pieces in a tureen, and pouring over them the soup, which should be very thick of leeks (a purée of leeks the French would call it).

Time. – 4 hours. Average cost 1s 8p per quart or with a (poorer) stock 1s.

Seasonable in winter.

Sufficient for 10 persons.

Note – Without the fowl, the above, which would then be merely called Leek Soup, is very good, and also economical.

The Victorian dinner

But not all middle-class, nineteenth-century, European food and eating habits were so frugal. The rich and successful had a very different life style. Conspicuous expenditure on furniture, tableware and food were a sign of the family's success. A vivid picture of such extravagant display has been left in this spiteful account of a French dinner party by the Goncourt brothers.

The dinner was sumptuous, overwhelming. On opening a table napkin one's hand caught on the heavily embroidered initials and crest of the mistress of the house. These were repeated on the plates while the glasses disappeared beneath engravings. Silver weighted down the sideboard; big majolica plates hung on the walls like shields. Lines of baskets of fruit and truffled delicacies filled the centre of the table. The meal began with a turtle soup, with pieces of real turtle in it, then truffles, pheasants, asparagus, and a thicket of prawns from the Meuse. For wines there were Château Yquem, le Les-d'Estournel, le Château-Margaux, the choicest wines from the Rhine.

Sitting down to a lavish Victorian dinner in 1890.

In Britain, the Victorian evening dinner party became an important and highly formalised ritual. Vast quantities of food were presented at table and inevitably wasted. Until the 1880s dinners were served in the French manner; that is in two or three courses with the dishes for each course laid out on the table. This dinner menu, not (it was stressed) involving 'high class cookery' was suggested by Alexis Soyer in his *The Modern Housewife* which was written partly in the form of letters from an experienced housewife to a new bride.

Our small evening parties, say thirty persons, are as follows; everything is cold, although I know that the fashion has been progressing towards having hot removes. Our table on those occasions is, as you know, in the form of a horseshoe. . . . In the centre and at the head of the table I place a large Grouse-pie, of which by my recommendation, everybody partakes: I then on each of the wings have Fowls, Lobster Salads, Mayonnaises of Fowl, Ham, Tongue, cut in slices and dished over parsley ornamented with Aspic Jelly; and on the sideboard I have a fine piece of Sirloin of Beef, plain roasted, or an Aitch-bone of Beef or a Fillet of Veal. . . . With the sweets I generally place about twelve – four on each table, that is 4 Jellies, 2 Creams, 2 Bavaroises, 4 Iced Cabinet Puddings and Raised Dishes of small pastry, all of which are artistically disposed upon the table. The fruits are likewise placed on the table, they consist of simple Compotes, 6 of various kinds and 6 of Dried Fruit, Biscuits, Wafers and Cossacks, which last are getting very much out of fashion but are very amusing.

Of course, not all dinners consisted of only cold dishes. Francatelli in his *Cook's Guide* proposed a quite different menu for a dinner of six to eight people: a dinner smaller in numbers perhaps but not in the relative quantities provided for each guest.

Cressy Soup
Boiled Dublin Bay haddock and egg sauce

Remove
Boiled capon with broccoli and white sauce

Entrées
Mutton cutlets à la Réforme
Sweetbreads larded à la Jardinière

Second course
Roast pheasant
Macaroni au gratin
Punch jelly
Pear tartlet

Francatelli was a pupil of Carême's and was probably the most distinguished British chef of the nineteenth century. His recipe for mutton cutlets à la Réforme is typical of the strong French influence on fashionable cooking in Britain by the middle of the nineteenth century:

> Having trimmed the cutlets let them be bread crumbed by first dipping them in beaten egg and then bread crumbing them in equal parts of dried bread crumbs and finely chopped lean ham mixed together: the cutlets must be fried on both sides, and when thoroughly done are to be dished up in a circle, the centre garnished with reform chips [see below]; and pour some reform sauce [see below] over the cutlets and serve.

Reform chips were composed of boiled carrots, black truffles, lean boiled ham, the whites of hard boiled eggs and the outsides of green gherkins, all neatly sliced into thin strips about $\frac{1}{2}$ inch (1 cm) long. These were warmed in a basin before being tossed together and piled in the centre of the dish. The sauce was made from 1 ounce of diced ham, carrot, celery and onion, together with a bay leaf, thyme, twenty peppercorns and a pinch of ground mace, all gently fried in a little butter until they were well browned. Then a wine glass of vinegar, half a glass of mushroom ketchup and 1 teaspoonful of anchovy essence was added and allowed to boil down to about half. Then half a pint brown sauce (or good stock and a little beurre manié) and a glass of sherry were stirred in and the pan set over a very gentle heat to simmer. When the fat had been skimmed off, the sauce was strained and returned to a clean pan. A glass of port, half a glass of sherry, 1 teaspoonful of anchovy essence and 2 good tablespoons of redcurrant jelly were mixed in and the sauce gently boiled for 5 minutes before being served with the cutlets.

The recipe for Reform sauce to be served with lamb cutlets was repeated as a standard classic dish in Escoffier's *Guide to Modern Cooking* first published in 1907 and republished as recently as 1977.

The presentation of the dishes at a Victorian dinner was highly elaborate, the result of plentiful cheap labour in the kitchen. Diners helped themselves and their neighbours to the dishes nearest them, or they could ask a waiter to fetch a particular dish from another part of the table. Inevitably meals took a long time and, in rooms without central heating, hot food was often cold by the time it reached the diner's plate. Towards the end of the century the introduction of 'Russian service' simplified the manner of serving dinner.

The kitchen at Lathom House, Lancashire, in the 1880s. The kitchen staff are all assembled and dishes of food can even be seen in the foreground.

Under this system the courses were clearly separated. Dishes were placed in turn on a sideboard and served to the guests by the waiters. Although served in more courses, fewer dishes and faster service resulted. Foods, served more quickly from the kitchen, gave chefs more scope for creating elaborate hot dishes which would have been spoilt by standing around. At the same time meals became more structured and the familiar modern pattern of soup, fish, entrée, roast, game, cheese and dessert emerged.

The British pudding

The French traveller M. Misson wrote of a visit to England in the 1690s:

> The pudding is a dish very difficult to be described, because of several sorts there of it: flour, milk, eggs, butter, sugar, suet, marrow, raisins etc etc are the most common ingredients of a pudding. They bake them in

an oven, or they boil them with meat, they make them fifty several ways: BLESSED BE HE THAT INVENTED PUDDING, for it is a manna that hits the palates of all sorts of people; a manna, better than that of the wilderness, because people are never weary of it. Ah, what an excellent thing is an English pudding!

Nearly 300 years later Elisabeth Ayrton in her *The Cookery of England* regretted 'these almost vanished splendours of our tables'.

Puddings started to become popular during the seventeenth century and by the end of the eighteenth century the choice was overwhelming. Sugar was no longer the exclusive luxury of the few and the general population of Britain were acquiring their modern addiction to sugar, either in their tea or in puddings and desserts. By 1800 the annual consumption of sugar per head in Britain had risen to over 30 pounds, although during the following twenty years it fell to around 20 pounds. Sweet dishes in medieval times, when sugar was precious, were served alongside savoury ones in the course of a banquet. During the seventeenth century cooked sweet dishes slowly became established as a regular feature of a meal, and were usually served with other savoury dishes in the second course. Meals often ended with fruit and confectionery as a final course. By the mid-nineteenth century the tradition of a full course of sweet cooked dishes at the end of the meal became firmly established.

At the beginning of the seventeenth century recipes for different fruit pies, fools, creams, syllabubs and fritters appeared in the printed cookery books together with a few baked and boiled puddings. But English puddings were transformed by the introduction of the boiling cloth soon after the end of the sixteenth century. Hitherto boiled puddings, the sweet and spicy versions of sausages and savoury puddings, were cooked in animals' guts. These had to be fresh, so boiled puddings could only be made during the season of the autumn slaughter of livestock. However, once boiled puddings had broken away from the limitations imposed by the need for fresh gut and were wrapped in a cloth, they could be cooked at any time of year. By the middle of the century wooden bowls were also in use as the directions 'boyle it either in a cloath, or in wooden dishes well buttered' show.

Quaking, or shaking, puddings of cream, breadcrumbs, sugar and eggs flavoured with spices were cooked in a well-floured bag in simmering water, apple puddings of apples, sugar and butter were wrapped in pastry skin and

A grotesque picture by Thomas Rowlandson (1756–1827) entitled A Good Meal. *To follow the enormous joint of meat already on the table, a maidservant is bringing in a boiled plum pudding.*

boiled in a cloth. The boiled suet pudding of the eighteenth century became the stereotype of the British pudding, regarded by foreigners as a national dish. Over the following centuries suet puddings developed and changed to meet the varying tastes and fashions of the times, until today the suet pudding has become part of the national Christmas binge. At its simplest a suet pudding was made with flour, suet, milk and possibly eggs and, until the middle of the nineteenth century, sometimes boiled in the same pot as the meat of the day. Eliza Acton in 1845 described it as shaped like a pastry roller, folded in a

A STRUGGLE WITH A PUDDING.

Girls in a school cookery class of 1891 learn how to boil a pudding tied in a cloth.

floured cloth tied tightly at the ends and said that 'in Kentish farmhouses and at very plain family dinners this pudding is usually sent to table with boiled beef and is sometimes cooked with it also.' In *Lark Rise to Candleford*, Flora Thompson described how at the end of the nineteenth century in her Oxfordshire village, 'Everything was cooked in the one utensil; the square of bacon, amounting to little more than a taste each; cabbage or other green vegetables in one net, potatoes in another, and the roly-poly swathed in a cloth'. The roly-poly pudding, sometimes with dried fruit in it, was served as a first course, (like its cousin the Yorkshire pudding) to take 'the edge off the appetite'. Such puddings survived into the twentieth century, flaccid pale rolls known to generations of school children as 'dead baby'. Other more attractive suet puddings were flavoured with ginger or lemon peel, or made with brown bread and served with a sherry sauce. Plum puddings enriched with dried fruits were already popular in the seventeenth century although they were not an established Christmas delicacy until the following century. They came in various forms; some were rich with fruits, sugar and spices such as cinnamon, nutmeg, ginger, cloves and mace, others economised by using dried fruit in place of sugar as a sweetener and omitting the spices, as in this seventeenth-century recipe for 'a plum pudding Boyled' from Rebecca Price's manuscript, published in *The Compleat Cook*.

> Take a peny lofe and pare off ye crust, then slice the crume very thine, and poure to it boyling hott a pinte of good milke, or creame, cover it up close and let it stand awhile to soake, then break ye bred small, and grate in halfe a nuttmeg, break in 4 eggs whites and all, and beat it all together, puting in by degrees 2 good handfulls of fine flower, and then put in a full quarter of a pounde of suet choped small, and 3 quarters of a pound of curants and raysons together, stir all well together with a little salt, and boyle it either in a cloath, or in wooden dishes well buttered and boyle it 3 howers.

By the mid-nineteenth century this recipe had been cut down still further and its name changed. Mrs Beeton published this economical version of it under the name of half-pay pudding – an oblique reference to the custom of paying army or navy officers only half their pay when they were not on active service. The eggs have gone, and black treacle, a cheap alternative to sugar, is introduced, perhaps to please an increasing demand for sweetness.

HALF-PAY PUDDING

$\frac{1}{4}$ lb suet, $\frac{1}{4}$ lb currants, $\frac{1}{4}$ lb raisins, $\frac{1}{4}$ lb flour, $\frac{1}{4}$ lb breadcrumbs, 2 tablespoons treacle, $\frac{1}{2}$ pint of milk.

Chop the suet finely: mix the currants which should be nicely washed, and dried; the raisins, which should be stoned, the flour, breadcrumbs and treacle; moisten with the milk, beat up the ingredients until all are thoroughly mixed, put them into a buttered basin, and boil the pudding for $3\frac{1}{2}$ hours. Sufficient for 5 or 6 people.

Finally this pudding appears again as a contemporary recipe on the back of an envelope dated 1948, collected from two elderly ladies living in the Lake District. It had become yet more reduced by war-time shortages and food rationing. The suet was changed to dripping and a teaspoon of baking powder added to give it lightness. However on the good side it now had an ounce of candied peel.

HALF-PAY PUDDING, 1948

$\frac{1}{4}$ *lb flour*
$\frac{1}{4}$ *lb dripping*
$\frac{1}{4}$ *lb breadcrumbs*
$\frac{1}{4}$ *lb raisins*
$\frac{1}{4}$ *lb currants*
1 oz candied peel
2 tablespoons treacle
1 teaspoon baking powder
$\frac{1}{2}$ *pint milk*

Mix well together. Place in a greased basin, cover with greased paper and boil for 2 to 3 hours.

I recommend replacing the dripping with suet, using self-raising flour and brown breadcrumbs and omitting the baking powder. Using a pressure cooker can cut the cooking time.

Today, except at Christmas, the suet pudding is a thing of the past along with so many other traditional puddings. The subject of health warnings and shunned by those who watch their weight, it is almost unknown and yet in times when food was less plentiful, it was welcomed for its ability to give pleasure and fill hungry stomachs at little cost.

Food at its worst

For the working classes the first half of the nineteenth century was a time when a working man's wages often failed to meet the cost of a family's food. The 1840s were known as the hungry forties. The diet of the majority was stodgy and monotonous but sufficient in quantity, but for the minority it was hopelessly deficient in both quantity and nutriment. Almost half the children born in towns died before they reached five years of age, and of those who survived a high proportion grew up rickety, undernourished and sometimes deformed. They were badly housed in filthy unsanitary slums, often only one room to a family and without proper cooking facilities. Engels, describing the conditions of workers in Manchester in 1851, wrote that:

> the habitual food of the individual working-man naturally varies according to his wages. The better paid workers, especially those in whose families every member is able to earn something, have good food as long as this state of things lasts; meat daily and bacon and cheese for supper. Where wages are less, meat is used only two or three times a week, and the proportion of bread and potatoes increases. Descending gradually, we find the animal food reduced to a small piece of bacon cut up with the potatoes; lower still even this disappears, and there remain only bread, cheese, porridge and potatoes, until on the lowest round of the ladder, among the Irish, potatoes form the sole food. As an accompaniment weak tea with perhaps a little sugar, milk or spirits is universally drunk … where no tea is used, the bitterest poverty reigns.

A cottager brewing tea at the end of the eighteenth century.

A few years before Engels wrote this account of working-class diets, the destruction of the Irish potato crop by blight had brought famine to Ireland.

The food provided for the British army during the nineteenth century echoes the appalling living standards experienced by the lower classes at that time. At the beginning of the nineteenth century a soldier's daily ration, for which he was charged 6 pence, was 1 pound of bread and $\frac{3}{4}$ pound of meat. The facilities for cooking the food were as impoverished as the food itself. In army barracks two coppers for each company were provided, one for meat and one for vegetables, so the food could only be boiled. There were no canteens; men cooked for themselves. Time was allowed for two meals a day at 7.30 a.m. and 12.30 p.m. When he was overseas, where large numbers of British soldiers spent the majority of their time, the soldier's meat ration was usually either salt pork or salt beef, so for years on end the daily fare was boiled salt beef and potatoes or dry biscuits.

An account of life in the army in India, quoted by Caroline Steedman in *The Radical Soldier's Tale*, illustrates the soldiers' conditions very vividly. John Pearman was a sergeant in 1846 when he wrote:

> Where we lay down there were a Large Shallow Pond and into this we all went to drink there was horses Camels Elephants men Bullocks all at once the water nearly like treakle but down it went ... no rations to be got Each man would get two rupees and do the Best we could with. I and two others went into the Town to try and bye something to eat. But we could not get anything the natives had got-nothing ... I got a Rams Head with the wool on this we took back to camp and when we got Back we had a Pound of Elephants Cakes [dry biscuits] gave to Each man. I soon eat my Lot one of the men got an Earthen Pot as Large as a pail this we made use of we made a fire put water into it and put it on the Fire we then scorched the wool off the Head and washed it and put it into the Earthen pot to Cook. it had stewed about $2\frac{1}{2}$ hours ... received orders to Strike Tents and march ... A man named Williams tried to take out the Head When he broke the Pot and the Broth run on the ground he got the thanks of the Boys we then pull the Head to peices and the Lucky man got a peice it was so hot it burnt your mouth but we got it down and worked at the tents at the same time we had become use to ruff it.

'There is death in the pot'

The quotation, 'There is death in the pot' from the Book of Kings in the Bible, was the sub-title of the first scientific analysis of the quality of food in Britain. The *Treatise on Adulterations of Food and Culinary Poisons* was written by Frederick Accum, a German chemist from Hanover, in 1820. In it he publicised his discovery that almost all commercial food and drink were adulterated. Bakers bleached inferior grades of flour with alum to make white bread – dark bread was generally perceived as a sign of poverty while 'finer'

The adulteration of food as seen by Cruickshank in 'London Improvements', 1845.

white bread commanded a higher price. At the beginning of the nineteenth century bakers frequently not only bleached the flour but diluted it with ground peas and beans. Brewers used even more noxious and poisonous chemicals as substitutes for malt and hops which enabled them to dilute their beer with no loss of 'flavour'. An aged taste was added to new beer by means of sulphuric acid. Beer which had gone sour was 'revived' with ground oyster shells. Accum also revealed that milk thickened with arrowroot was sold as cream, the skins of Gloucester cheeses were coloured with red lead, the crusting of old port was imitated by lining the bottle with a layer of 'supertartrate of potash', and that large quantities of tea were manufactured from the British hedgerows. Leaves of blackthorn, ash and elder were boiled, dried and coloured on copper plates. It was estimated that nearly half of all the teas sold in Britain were fake. Coffee drinkers fared no better, since ground coffee was diluted with chicory and toasted corn. Accum made so many powerful enemies with the publication of his book, that after a somewhat spurious court case he was forced to leave the country in 1821.

If anything, during the next few decades, the adulteration of foods increased. By 1848 it was said to be impossible to find commercial bread that did not contain alum and often boiled potatoes as well. Flour itself was mixed with chalk, pipe-clay, powdered flints and potato flour. A flourishing trade had grown up in second-hand tea leaves. Used tea leaves were given as perks to the servants in grand houses who sold them to merchants. They in turn mixed the tea leaves with gum, dried and 'faced' them with black lead before selling them again as fresh tea leaves.

Why did adulteration of food grow to such proportions in the nineteenth century? The Victorians were no more evil-minded than earlier generations, in fact they are often seen as having higher ideals despite their hypocrisy. In previous centuries English bakers and brewers had been controlled by the Assizes of Bread and Ale which worked reasonably well in the small urban communities of the pre-industrial era. However, the medieval controls were on the weight and price of bread and the strength of beer; no provision was made for the adulteration of ingredients. In the rapidly growing cities of the early nineteenth century the organisation of any controls at all broke down, with the old Acts of Assize being repealed in 1815. In addition, this was coupled with a far wider knowledge of chemistry. The new century also brought a freer attitude to trade and commerce. Government no longer attempted to intervene between the producer, retailer and consumer to regulate the price or quality of food. It was not until the 1870s that anxiety about the health of people exposed to so much adulterated food finally moved Parliament to legislate against food adulteration. Even then it needed many court cases and attempts at publicising and banning such practices, before food health laws finally started to make progress in Britain in the twentieth century.

Steamships and railways

The great progress made in all forms of transportation during the nineteenth century directly affected the foods people ate. In the seventeenth and eighteenth centuries London and Paris had attracted expensive foods, such as oysters, good meat and wine, from several hundred miles away, but their delivery was limited by the size of loads that could be carried by horses or oxen on the rough and pot-holed roads, or carried slowly by canal or sea, or driven on the hoof. Food took time to reach its destination. At the end of the eighteenth century fresh salmon packed in ice was sent by fast carriages drawn by four horses from Scotland to London, but such swift transport was only for luxury foods. However, by the mid-nineteenth century not only were roads engineered and surfaced so that coaches carrying expensive items could travel faster, but with the opening up of the railway network great quantities of cheaper goods could be carried much further and faster. By 1860 almost all the mainline rail network in Great Britain was completed, while in America by about 1870 there were nine major routes linking the west coast with the south and east. Railways had a dramatic influence on the food of the growing cities, both in Europe and the USA. Before the coming of the railways a drive of longhorn cattle from the western United States to the east could involve 2500 animals travelling 1500 miles at speeds of between ten to twenty miles a day – up to five months' steady plodding. After the building of the railways meat supplies for cities no longer arrived on foot, but could be carried either live or as carcasses in refrigeration units in a fraction of the time. In the United States the trans-continental trains enabled the rich western lands to become the granary of Great Britain and the fear of frequent famines was finally banished from Europe.

At the end of the twentieth century specially designed long distance lorries and motorway networks have, to a large extent, replaced rail for the transport of food both in North America and Europe. Three-temperature lorries with normal, chill and frozen compartments can carry foods direct to the retail outlets. Perishable foods can be collected from the producers and delivered direct to the wholesaler some 1000 miles away in peak condition. Iceberg lettuces, strawberries and melons in refrigerated lorries travel from south-west France or Spain to northern England in twenty-four hours. Foods prepared in factories in the east of England can be on supermarket shelves in Edinburgh and Southampton by opening time the following morning. Californian fruits and vegetables are trucked to be sold fresh in British Columbia over 1000 miles away.

The new industrial technology of the nineteenth century also brought the invention of the steamship. During that century sailing ships eventually gave way to steamships, but not before the fast tea clippers had reduced the time taken from China to London to ninety-nine days. The journey from Canton could easily take six months or even more, with the ships trading *en route*. The opening of the Suez Canal in 1869 cut still further the time taken from the East to Europe. By the end of the century iron and steel construction had replaced wooden ships and the development of the expansion engine in the 1860s enabled steamships to carry both cargo and passengers economically. Finally with the invention of cold-storage ships, perishables could be shipped

The refrigerated hold of a merchant ship around 1887.

across the Atlantic and from Australia to Europe. These changes basically revolutionised British food. Farmers in Britain could not compete with meat from the vast tracts of land and huge herds of the Australian and Argentinian farmers. Frozen mutton and beef from Australia was about half the price of fresh British meat, and by the end of the century meat consumption in Britain had more than doubled since the 1860s. Nowadays refrigerated containers bring exotic fruits from South America to Europe in between two to three weeks and even the Japanese are exploring the possibilities of exporting fruit to North America.

Canning was another nineteenth-century industrial process which had a long-lasting effect on people's eating habits. Canned meats and vegetables had first been supplied to the Navy in 1813 but a series of bad production techniques which resulted in putrid meat did a great deal of harm to the growing industry and for a number of years people regarded canned meat with suspicion. But later in the century Mrs Beeton in her *Everyday Cookery* wrote of canned meat: 'the prejudice that some people entertained against these has now almost ceased to exist'. Canned beef was also even cheaper than the imported frozen beef. However, although according to Mrs Beeton canned beef 'is excellent and it is well worth while to try it for mulligatawny soup, or for a meat pudding ... It is also nice eaten cold with a salad', other accounts of it in the 1880s are perhaps more realistic. It came in big clumsy red tins. Inside the lean meat was coarse-grained and stringy, with a large lump of unpleasant looking fat on one side of it and the uneven hollows partly filled with a watery fluid.

Despite an inauspicious start, though, the techniques of canning progressed and canned fish and fruits brought a new variety of foods to many people. By the 1880s canned Californian pineapples and peaches were common in Britain and by 1914 she was the largest importer of canned foods. Canned salmon and canned peaches became the traditional Sunday tea for many people.

6

THE MODERN WORLD – *from* 1900 *to the* PRESENT DAY

A cause for concern

At the beginning of the twentieth century the British authorities were shocked to discover that 38 per cent of the volunteers for the Boer War had to be rejected on account of their poor physical condition – heart conditions, poor sight and hearing, bad teeth – and this was after the minimum height requirement of the recruits had been reduced to five feet. Similar results had been found in France at the start of the Franco-Prussian War in 1870. A number of private social surveys at the time revealed that a substantial proportion of working-class families could not maintain themselves in health on the wages they earned. Seebohm Rowntree in *Poverty*, his survey of York in 1899, found that 20 302 persons (43 per cent of the wage-earning classes and 28 per cent of the total population of the city) were living in such poverty that they did not have the money to purchase enough food to keep them 'physically efficient'. These revelations finally shocked the government into action. A committee on Physical Deterioration was set up and parliamentary Acts providing free school meals for children of poor families and pensions for the elderly marked the start of the state's acceptance of responsibility for the health and wellbeing of the people.

At the beginning of World War I knowledge of nutrition had progressed sufficiently to enable the authorities to calculate the calorific value of different foods in the national diet. The existence of carbohydrates and proteins in different foods and their function in diet had been discovered during the nineteenth century by European scientists. By 1900 scientists were gradually isolating foods containing different vitamins and identifying their uses to the

Free meals for poor children. Only spoons were provided until the 1930s.

human body, although it was to be another twenty years before their chemical composition was known. British working-class diet in 1914 was dominated by bread, sugar, lard, cheese, bacon and condensed milk. Usually the meat they bought was either chilled from Argentina or frozen from New Zealand; both were cheaper than home-produced meat. Working people had little leeway in their diets. Ironically, wartime price controls, together with full employment, allowed many working people a better diet than they had ever previously enjoyed. When food rationing came in 1918 it did not reduce consumption as a whole, but roughly levelled out the patterns of consumption in the country and across social classes. It also established that Government had a part to play in the regulation of the people's nutrition.

The midday dinner

Although the English upper crust in the nineteenth and early twentieth century dined at night, for the great majority of both working- and middle-class families the main hot meal of the day, also called dinner, was eaten in the middle of the day. With industrialisation came the question of where and when the workers ate their meals during working hours. Before the growth of factories and the change in style and scale of employment, numbers of workers were smaller and meal breaks tended to be more domestic – often the master craftsman provided the midday meal for his workers as was also customary on many farms. But this changed with the coming of the factories. Working hours in the factories were very long – fourteen or more hours a day was usual, with people working eighty hours or more in a week. In the 1840s work in the Staffordshire potteries could start at five o'clock in the morning and go on to nine or ten at night; the dinner break lasted an hour between one and two, and from then onwards there were no more meal breaks until work stopped in the evenings. At a 'good' cotton mill in Manchester the working day started at six in the morning and went on to eight at night; the workers were allowed an hour for dinner at noon, half an hour for breakfast and another half hour during the afternoon. Other employers provided no set meal breaks and workers had to find what time and space they could to eat at their work.

Gradually during the century the provisions for industrial workers' welfare improved and by the 1890s some enlightened employers, such as Cadbury's, Colman's, Fry's and Lever Brothers, were providing their workers with canteens where they could buy a hot meal. At the Cadbury's works at Bourneville in 1905 a dinner of roast meat and two vegetables from the canteen cost fourpence. However, for the majority of industrial workers there was no canteen at work until after 1940, although some employers provided a room where workers could eat away from their work, and sometimes facilities to heat their own food. Shops, where the working hours were often even longer than in industry, made little provision for their workers' refreshment – an exception to this were some big London departmental stores where young single workers who 'lived in' had a canteen which provided them with a midday meal. During the first decade of this century Marks and Spencers in Leeds, at midday, only provided tea and two canteen cookers on which the girls could warm food they brought from home.

By 1910 the food taken to work for midday meals might be a pie or a basin of meat and vegetable stew to be re-heated, or cold sandwiches of corned beef or bacon, together with the wherewithal for a hot drink – a spoonful of tea leaves mixed with a spoonful of sweetened condensed milk wrapped in a screw of paper. Yorkshire miners working in the high temperatures underground in the 1930s took a bottle of cold tea in one pocket and a 'snap' tin of sandwiches in the other. They had no set meal break but ate as they worked 'for there is no comfort or satisfaction underground'. Some workers in big cities bought meals from hot food stalls. An elderly Birmingham resident remembers:

> ... there were a lot of small factories round the market and everywhere in Birmingham ... as I remember, meat and two veg and a sweet – 6d.; and the work people used to go and have that, it saved a lot of trouble. [In Birmingham market] there was a place, it was about three or perhaps four stalls in one and it was where they did cooked meals, and they used to start about 12 o'clock I think it was, and the chap there he used to stand on trestles, sort of thing, higher up, and they had a big dish of lamb, beef and pork and he used to carve whichever meat you wanted; a lamb dinner, cost you 10d. with two veg, and beef cost you 11d. and if you wanted pork with crackling on, that was 1/- ... that was Charlie Miles.

This was an expensive meal in the 1920s when the average worker's wage was around thirty shillings per week.

Miles' food stall in Birmingham market. The customers sat on high stools at the counter with the roast joints on hot plates in front of them. A list of prices hangs above.

Lunch on the factory floor.

Other workers went home either from preference or economy – as late as 1938 over 50 per cent of husbands ate their midday meal at home. The hot midday dinner was invariably meat, potatoes and vegetables – often root vegetables, or dried peas or beans, with pudding and tea. In the new towns which grew up out of the old industrial villages, workers lived close to the factories, but as the nineteenth century progressed demand for houses spread them further from the factory gates, although usually still within walking distance. By the end of the century many people were living a tram ride away from work. For many of those who went home for their meal the midday break meant a tight schedule – one wife watched to see her husband cross a nearby bridge, then by the time he arrived at the door his food had to be on the table.

In some families, particularly in the northern industrial towns, a child would be sent to the factory gates with a hot dinner for the father. This sometimes involved a tram ride – but a child travelled half fare – and it enabled the father to have a hot midday meal. An account from an old lady in Birmingham described how in the 1920s her father's dinner would be in a basin covered with a plate and wrapped in a towel and she would catch a tram for a half-penny ride and then walk for ten minutes to the factory where her father would be waiting; afterwards she would get back home and have her own dinner before going back to school. The school dinner hour was typically one and a half hours long, perhaps to accommodate such duties.

A typical dish which might have been carried to the factory is this beef steak pudding. The recipe, dated 18 October 1911, was used in a school domestic science lesson in Stockport.

BEEF STEAK PUDDING

Line greased basin with suet paste, put in the filling, half fill with water, cover with paste, tie a scalded and floured cloth over, put into boiling water and boil from $3\frac{1}{2}$ to 4 hours.

Paste
$\frac{1}{4}$ *lb flour*
2 ozs suet
$\frac{1}{4}$ *teaspoon salt*
$\frac{1}{4}$ *teaspoon Baking Powder*
cold water

Method
Chop suet, mix flour, salt and BP, form into paste with cold water and use.

Filling
$\frac{1}{4}$ *lb shoulder steak*
1 teaspoon flour
$\frac{1}{4}$ *teaspoon salt*
pepper

Mix flour, pepper and salt, cut meat into small pieces, toss in flour and use.

There were many Victorian middle-class efforts at improving the lot of the working classes including the provision of cookery classes in schools in the 1890s. Unfortunately, the recipes taught in these classes were often more suitable for upper-class dinner parties than working-class homes. Although the beef steak pudding recipe was eminently suitable in its time; it seems very stodgy and heavy to modern taste.

The tradition of hot midday dinners depended on someone, often the wife, being at home to prepare and cook a meal. After 1945 came a change. Increasingly wives joined the work force and were no longer at home themselves. People lived much further away from their workplaces and the time taken in getting to work increased for most of the population. Gradually the midday meal lost its importance, although many canteens still find that 'meat and two veg.' is their most popular meal, particularly for people doing heavy manual work. For office and other sedentary workers the midday meal has been largely overtaken by the snack, and the main hot meal of the day has been pushed back to the evening. A quick snack can save working time – when time is precious – just as a main meal bought ready prepared saves leisure time. The demand for a quick lunch snack has opened the way for fast foods, while convenience foods have developed to meet the needs for an easily prepared evening meal at the end of a working day. The move away from midday meals has been supported by recent nutritional thinking which suggests that the energy required to digest a full dinner could more profitably be spent on work during the afternoon. Post-1945 ideas of healthy eating have also strengthened moves against the perceived stodgy foods of the pre-War dinner.

In Britain there appears to be a growing polarisation of main eating occasions between weekdays and weekends with traditional meals declining. Midweek meals are dominated by fast food and convenience foods, while the hot midday dinner at home is almost a thing of the past. Traditional cooked meals have been elevated into special occasions at the weekends, now often demanding exotic and expensive ingredients. Sunday lunch is still a feature in many households but increasingly the fashion is to eat it out.

Other countries are going through changes too. In America it has long been the practice for the main meal to be eaten after the end of work with a light lunch or snack at midday. Fast food outlets such as hotdog stalls, pizza parlours and McDonalds opened to supply this need. Schoolchildren take sandwiches and snacks from home for their midday break. However, in Europe the midday tradition is dying much more slowly. In Germany it is customary to eat a big meal at midday either at home, in a small restaurant or in the works' canteen and then come home to a light supper of cheeses and cold meats. The main meal in Switzerland is still eaten in the middle of the day; people at work usually eat in small, often unlicensed restaurants or in works' canteens. In Switzerland it is customary for mothers with school-age children not to go out to work and the children come home for their midday meal. Throughout France small restaurants are filled at midday with people eating three-course meals and most French secondary schools provide a full meal at midday. But it is no longer as common as it was forty years ago for the main midday meal to be cooked at home during the week. Sunday lunch in France is an occasion for family gatherings, either at home for an elaborate meal, or sometimes in a restaurant with the whole family spending several hours eating a five- or six-course meal.

Food in wartime

During World War II food for ordinary people in Britain was tightly rationed. Bitter memories of the inequalities and shortages during the previous war developed into an 'obsession' with profiteering, which in turn influenced the Government into establishing strict price controls. It also produced a climate of opinion in favour of rationing before shortages really developed. Just as during World War I the state policy for controlling prices and rationing essential foods, meant that the nutritional standards of many working families actually rose, although for the more prosperous families, wartime food became unutterably dreary.

Butter and bacon were rationed in November 1939, and were joined by meat and sugar in December. The following year tea and margarine were added to the list. By July 1940 additional shortages of cheese, eggs, milk, jam and sweets brought them into the rationing system. By spring 1941 there was some talk of malnutrition. In 1941 a points system was introduced which, from the beginning, was popular with the public. At first tinned meats, tinned fish and dried beans were on points, then dried fruits, breakfast cereals and biscuits were added. At the beginning of each month each consumer was issued with a number of 'points' which could be spent according to preference upon what was available. Foods were priced in 'points' as well as money and this gave a sense of choice.

Everyone was issued with ration books and was required to register with their grocer, butcher and dairyman for basic rations. The amounts of the weekly rations varied according to the season and the state of national food stocks and they were announced each month. Rations were strictly calculated to ensure that the population remained healthy, even if not well fed. The science of nutrition had made great progress since World War I, and by 1939 it was possible to plan diets from limited food supplies. Meat was rationed by price at between 1 to 2 shillings a week per person – about 5 pounds' weight a week for a family of five. Often some of the ration was in the form of corned beef. The bacon ration fluctuated between 4 ounces and 8 ounces weekly while the rations for fat – which included butter, margarine and lard – and for cheese could be as low as 1 ounce a week rising to 8 ounces in some months. Milk and eggs also varied with the season. Between 8 ounces and 1 pound of sugar and 2 to 4 ounces of tea were also standard rations, although extra sugar was allocated for jam-making in the autumn. There were extra rations for manual workers, young children and pregnant mothers. This system of controlling a limited number of food items provided a diet of around 3000 calories daily for British manual workers; the Germans in World War II used a system of total rationing which allowed a diet of around 2600 calories for their manual workers.

It was British Government policy to allow sufficient 'filling' food so that no one need feel hungry. Bread was not rationed until after the end of the war. It was subsidised, as it had been at the end of World War I. The national

Advertisements and slogans to encourage the use of potatoes during World War II were frequently issued by the Ministry of Food. People were advised to use potatoes to eke out the meagre meat rations, as sandwich fillings, and in place of pastry for flans and pie tops, as well as a substitute for suet in steamed puddings.

wholemeal loaf was introduced, made from a flour milled to include 85 per cent of the grain, rising to 90 per cent. This was, however, considered by many to be a grey dreary bread. Potatoes were never rationed. Schoolchildren were encouraged to help with the lifting and clamping of potatoes in the autumn as they were with the picking of fruit during the summer.

Meals were planned more carefully than they had been before the war. People ate unfamiliar foods; jokes were made about snoek – a kind of fish – and whale meat and spam, a canned meat from the States, bought on 'points'. It is said that in 1956 President Eisenhower gave the production company which produced spam a Presidential pardon for inflicting it on the American army. Recipes abounded for its use. This recipe for barbecued spam, taken from a family notebook, was a party piece for entertaining visitors.

BARBECUED SPAM

1 tin spam
cloves
5 tablespoons sugar
1 dessertspoon water
1 large teaspoon made mustard
1 dessertspoon vinegar

Put the spam in a shallow baking dish. Score the top and insert cloves. Bake in a moderate oven for 10 minutes. Mix the sugar, mustard, vinegar and water together and pour over the spam. Bake for another 20 minutes, basting frequently.

Dried milk and dried eggs took the place of fresh milk and eggs, requiring new recipes for their satisfactory use. Dried milk had to be carefully mixed with water to avoid it going lumpy and dried eggs always tasted of cardboard. Fish and fruit were not rationed but were often in very short supply. A rumour would spread that a certain shop had fresh fish or oranges and people would hurry to join the queue. In effect, shops often organised their own rationing systems for regular customers only, to discourage people from joining queues and ensure that regular customers had a share in whatever was available.

An example of the kind of recipes used by housewives during the war is this fruit cake which also comes from a family notebook. It was a great favourite because, unlike many wartime cakes which were dry from the lack of eggs, this cake was moist.

FRUIT CAKE

8 oz flour
1 teaspoon bicarbonate of soda
1 teaspoon spice
4 oz sugar
4 oz fat
4 oz dried fruit
1 teacup strong tea

Boil fat, fruit and tea for 3 minutes. Cool and add to the dry ingredients. Beat well. Bake in a moderate oven for $1\frac{1}{2}$ hours.

The authorities in wartime were not only concerned with rations and shortages but also the problems of feeding those left homeless in the air raids. Margaret Broatch, who was responsible for emergency feeding in London at the beginning of the Blitz in 1940, wrote to her mother in the country describing how she was struggling to feed those who had lost their homes:

> ... my whole time is being taken up with feeding the homeless – we tried at first to do them from the Central Kitchens (which before the war were responsible for the school meals service) but it was almost impossible to get the meal to the various rest centres in time firstly because so many roads are closed for time bombs or craters in the road and the traffic has

to be diverted. Secondly for the first few days Air Raids coincided with meals. I should have explained that people who have lost their homes are taken into rest shelters which may be in a school, these are 1st line places and are filled first, or into Church halls etc. They get breakfast, tea and supper on the premises, but have to be provided with a hot meal midday. The transport question was so grave that I had to look round for some other means of dealing with the situation...

As a result the author arranged for domestic science teachers to cook meals in the schools.

... I sent in more equipment and the staff did the work. I now have about 32 centres cooking on the spot and the Central Kitchens doing the rest. That all worked until the gas failed, Townsend Street was without gas for two weeks, so I had to get field kitchens and boilers going in the school yards and now we have a fairly good service and were getting on merrily until Tuesday, when after a very bad night our numbers trebled and Trinity Street (one of the rest centres) needed 3200 meals. They

Mobile boilers, like this one in the East End of London, provided hot water for people who had neither water nor gas as a result of the bombing in 1940–1.

however were without gas and water, so I had to get some fed by mobile canteens, (Trinity Street did 1900, pretty good!) and they did all eventually get a meal.

'Blitz stew' of meat, vegetables and potatoes with bread and margarine and tea was a typical midday meal served by these emergency kitchens. Raynes Minns in her book *Bombers and Mash* quotes the ingredients necessary for 'Emergency Meal No. 2 for 100 people for cooking in large air raid shelters, field kitchens, British restaurants.'

> 10 lb meat (bully beef etc.)
> 5 lb haricot beans
> 10 lb onions or leeks
> 20 lb carrots
>   (or 30 lb of any mixed vegetables)
> 65 lb potatoes
> 1 lb oatmeal or wheatmeal flour
> 1 lb parsley (chopped)
> water or stock
> 1 lb cooking fat
> 25 lb wheatmeal bread
> 1½ lb margarine

A note at the bottom adds 'this stew can be cooked in a clean dustbin after an air raid emergency.' Anyone having such a meal would feel full although the allowance of only 1½ ounces of meat per person might have made the gravy seem rather thin to modern tastes.

A soldier's food

The organisation of army food supplies had probably not improved from the time of the Romans until after the end of the eighteenth century. Although it was recognised that an army marched on its stomach and depended on its food supplies, in practice, in the stress of war, supplies failed and soldiers were forced to rely on what they could find locally for their food. At Valley Forge in the winter of 1777 during the American War of Independence the rebel soldiers were hungry, often without meat and always without vegetables because the supply system had broken down; some days they went without food altogether. The officers at Valley Forge suffered no such privations and were able to supplement their rations from their own pockets. George Washington who was the Commander-in-Chief ran up a bill of thousands of dollars for the wines drunk while he was entertaining official visitors during that winter.

During the American Civil War in the 1860s the North had better communications, and in particular more railway lines, than the Southern confederacy. Although officially soldiers on both sides had the same rations – $1\frac{1}{4}$ pounds fresh meat or $\frac{3}{4}$ pound salt pork, sugar, salt, coffee, and hard tack made from flour, water, baking powder, salt and oil – the North's ability to supply their soldiers was crucial to their final victory. In Europe during the Crimean War a British soldier recalled returning to the camp after a day in the field around Sebastopol 'to a cold bleak muddy tent, without fire and often not even a piece of mouldy biscuit to eat, nothing served out yet'. Officers fared better, as this letter written by a young officer, Lieutenant Richards, from the siege of Sebastopol in October 1854 and quoted in Christopher Hibbert's book *The destruction of Lord Raglan*, shows: 'We get 1 pd. of biscuit and $\frac{3}{4}$ pds. of pork [salt] or 1 pd. of fresh meat per day and a $\frac{1}{4}$ of a gill of rum ... not much you will say to live on, but we manage by foraging to eke it out with cabbage, turnips, fowls, pumpkins, water melons and grapes.'

The British army had arrived at the Black Sea with no transport and no supplies and came close to defeat as a result. The commissary had expected to hire local mules but these were unobtainable. Lieutenant Richards wrote that:

Piles of stores, boxes, sacks, bundles of hay, lay in muddled heaps on the quayside, ... Overworked commissariat officers picked their way through the muddle with bundles of forms and requisitions ... badgered at every corner by enraged regimental officers, who hated and despised them ... and who accused them of all manner of dishonesty and neglect ... When anything is applied for you find Mr. Commissary Jones, Smith or Robinson smoking a cigar ... who tells you that really he is very sorry he believes that the article is somewhere in one of the stores, but where it is he has not the slightest idea, and at present he has no time to look for it.

Alexis Soyer reformed the provision of hospital food for sick and wounded soldiers in the Crimea as well as designing a mobile stove contraption for the British army.

At the end of the Spanish-American War, fought by the Americans in Mexico and the Philippines at the end of the nineteenth century, the United States authorities were appalled to discover that for every soldier that had died in the field, fourteen had died in camp from illness or malnutrition. There was a thorough reorganisation of the US army supply and feeding systems with the result that by 1917 during World War I the army had mobile kitchens – known as slum burners – which could be brought up close to the front lines and provide hot meals for the troops in the trenches. The hot food was placed in a kind of insulated food carrier which retained heat for up to eighteen hours, and distributed to the troops in the trenches. Towards the end of the war individual soldiers also had small stoves with solidified alcohol on which they could prepare hot drinks.

By the start of World War II army catering had made great strides aided partly by new industrial technology. Canned pork meat, such as spam, and dried milk and coffee became part of army rations. In the British army, real improvements came in 1941 with the formation of the Army Catering Corps and the organisation of army cooks and kitchens. Composite Rations, sufficient to provide twelve men with breakfast, dinner, evening meal and snacks, were issued for use in the field. These were made up of canned meat, puddings, biscuits, cheese, chocolate, tea, sugar and milk powder and replaced the old tin of meat, packet of biscuits and piece of cheese provided by the old-style army emergency rations. Every British soldier had a mess tin in which food could be cooked and some attempts, although not very convincing, were made to train soldiers to be self-reliant – during training in 1944, for instance, they were issued with a mutton chop and a potato in place of the evening meal and expected to get on with it.

A soldier enjoying a hot meal from a mobile food carrier in World War I.

American soldiers were issued with a different kind of emergency rations. D-rations supplied to the US army for the Normandy landings in June 1944 consisted of high-calorific chocolate bars fortified with vitamins, devised by the Hershy Company in America; three bars could provide sufficient food for one day. Before the end of the war came K-rations, issued to the British army as well as the Americans. These packs, about the size of a packet of biscuits, contained a small can of meat, a powdered-milk drink, biscuits, toilet paper, cigarettes, chewing gum and a fruit bar or sweets.

During the war in Vietnam other emergency packs were devised: C-rations were a daily ration of 3500 calories made up of canned meats, such as pork or turkey, canned peaches or other fruits, salt, pepper, matches, chewing gum and cigarettes – the latter were later abolished in the anti-smoking moves of the 1970s. It was said that one reason for the American defeat in Vietnam was the ability of the Viet Cong to live on a reduced and 'lean' diet while the American forces needed to carry around a great weight of food.

War and industry have tended to go together in the originating and development of new techniques. Hershy bars of dark, semi-sweet chocolate, spam and instant coffee flourished in the needs of World War II. Freeze-dried coffee was the product of the Korean war. Recent new and improved dehydrated and extruded foods, such as pot noodles, give much lighter rations to soldiers, while inventions such as heat tabs enabled individual soldiers to heat food without recourse to an open fire. Even these, a product of the seventies, have been superseded by flameless ration heaters – chemical pads activated by water which can heat a meal in five minutes.

Quick and easy

Today's eating habits have changed dramatically from those we have seen through the ages. Today the fourteenth-century recipe for squid and onion rings given in *Le Ménagier de Paris* would read something like this: take one packet frozen battered squid rings and one packet frozen deep-fried onion rings. Cook according to the instructions on the packet and serve with aïoli sauce, bought ready-prepared. This last item does not perhaps differ so much from the original, for *Le Ménagier* also recommended buying sauces ready-made from the sauce-maker. Households today, where all the adults are often in full-time work outside the home, need midweek meals that can be put onto the table quickly and with as little effort as possible. The food industry has responded to these needs with a rapidly increasing range of convenience foods. Gone are dishes made at home from recipes demanding lengthy and detailed preparation with numerous ingredients. Many of today's meals are blended and flavoured in the laboratories of the food industry. The modern housewife can buy a wide range of aids towards producing fast meals ranging from cook-in-sauces for use with unprocessed meats, through prepared dishes needing some cooking such as breaded and battered fish and chicken portions, to the full-blown ready-prepared pre-cooked dinner requiring only heating. Domestic freezers and microwave ovens enlarge still further the working housewife's control of when and how she cooks a meal. Recipes themselves are changing with these advances. Many now make use of prepared and processed foods leaving the housewife to do only the final blending. This recipe, clearly illustrating this trend, comes from a Canadian cookbook *Royal Treats for Entertaining*.

SEAFOOD SCALLOP SHELLS

A perfect make ahead. All ingredients can be combined, placed in shells and frozen without cooking. Just thaw and bake to serve.

1 × 10 oz can cream of celery soup
$\frac{1}{4}$ *cup milk*
1 beaten egg
$\frac{1}{4}$ *cup Parmesan cheese*
1 × 5 oz can of crab meat, flaked
1 × 4$\frac{1}{4}$ oz can shrimp, rinsed and drained
1 × 10 oz can sliced mushrooms, drained
$\frac{1}{4}$ *cup fine bread crumbs*
1 tablespoon melted butter

Combine soup, milk, beaten egg and 2 tablespoons cheese in saucepan. Stir over low heat till hot. Add seafood and mushrooms. Spoon into one large casserole or four large shells.

Melt butter. Add last 2 tablespoons cheese and bread crumbs. Sprinkle over seafood mixture. Bake at 375° F for 30 minutes.

This recipe may be doubled.

The new foods on supermarket or grocery store shelves have been made possible by the tremendous advances made by the food industry in food technology and food science over the last twenty-five years. The development of cook-chill dishes so suited to busy life styles have transformed the 'ready meals' market in Britain. It has been estimated that at the beginning of 1989 over 400 000 such packs were sold daily.

Another great technological advance has been the development of extrusion cooking. This system enables a moistened, starchy material, made partly from soya beans, to be cooked in a tube under pressure. This de-natures the proteins so that the material can be stretched and restructured. The resulting dough is then forced through openings in a die to shape it into thin ropes which can then be cut, shaped and dried as required. This highly technical process has produced such disparate foods as pot noodles, vitamin-enriched breakfast cereals, textured vegetable protein, oven-ready potato chips, and numerous cheese-flavoured snacks.

The advances in food technology have been made possible to a large extent by changes in retailing patterns which have transformed grocery shopping since World War II. Before the war many people bought from small corner grocery shops with a limited range of goods on offer, mainly dry and tinned goods together with bacon, butter and cheese. They had little refrigeration or storage capacity and like Asian shops today they stayed open until late at night. Careful customers delayed shopping until late on Saturday evening when meats and other perishables, which would not keep over the weekend, were reduced in price. Others bought from multiple grocers, such as the Co-op (mostly in the North), Lipton's or Sainsbury's (in the South). The first successful Co-op shop opened in Rochdale in 1844 and sold small quantities of butter, sugar, flour, oatmeal, and candles. It opened two evenings a week with the Co-op Society committee members serving as salespersons. The following year it opened every night and had added tea and tobacco to its stock. By 1900 there

A village general store in the late 1940s. Like the corner shops in towns, village stores stocked a range of dry and canned goods, butter, bacon and cheese.

were 1439 retail Co-op Societies and by 1939 the Co-op was often the biggest shop in a northern town. Thomas Lipton opened his first grocery shop in Scotland in 1871 and by the 1890s had established shops in most big towns in the United Kingdom. They sold only a limited number of items – flour, sugar, butter, bacon, cheese, dried peas and beans, condensed milk and, after 1889, tea – mainly to working-class customers. The Sainsbury's chain grew from a dairy in Drury Lane opened by J. J. Sainsbury in 1869. These shops were aimed at a more middle-class clientele in the London suburbs and carried a wider range of goods. Most dry foods such as biscuits, sugar, and dried fruits came to the shops in bulk and were weighed and packed individually for each customer. Sainsbury's in particular made a point of cutting butter from the large 'casks' which stood on the marble counters and shaping each order into a neat block between two wooden butter 'hands' in front of the customer. The retailing of other foods was much more specialised: cooked-meat shops sold ham, boiled mutton and roast beef, all sliced cold; pork butchers were distinct from general butchers who might or might not also be poulterers; fishmongers often sold only fish; small bakers sold their own fresh-baked bread and buns while cake shops, sometimes serving morning coffee or afternoon teas, sold cakes; dairies sold milk, cream and eggs; while grocers never sold meat, fish, fruit or vegetables. Self-service stores first appeared in Britain in 1949 and were followed by the supermarket as we now know it in the 1960s.

Sainsbury's Guildford branch in 1906 was stocked with a wide range of different cheeses, bacon, ham and sausages as well as tea and some tinned goods.

In 1990 supermarkets controlled almost 70 per cent of the British food and drink trade and handled up to 80 per cent of the major food manufacturers' output. These big retailers have the power and the economic resources to shape and respond to consumer demand in ways that would have been impossible for the small pre-war shops. They also devote many of their resources to creating a demand for new products which compete with traditional ones and so hopefully generate more trade. They can demand packaging to suit their particular selling and display needs, such as vacuum packs for bacon which stack easily, have good visibility and give the bacon a prolonged shelf-life without discolouring.

Shelf-life is of great importance to the big retailer carrying large supplies and to consumers shopping only once a week. Much research has gone into prolonging the keeping time of foods. There has been a great deal of discussion world-wide about food irradiation which if applied to fruit and vegetables greatly increases their keeping quality. This is a process which employs ionising energy in the form of gamma rays, electrons or X-rays to destroy insects, parasites, and micro-organisms which cause disease. The process also slows down the physiological process of ripening and maturing in a number of foods such as soft fruits like strawberries. Some countries allow a limited use of these techniques, others do not. Spices, which are particularly prone to invasion by parasites and insects, are irradiated in the USA and many European countries. From January 1991 irradiated foods have been allowed in the UK provided they are clearly marked as irradiated. Some supermarkets have said they will not sell such foods.

Safe foods

Highly processed foods occupy a major part of the grocery trade throughout the industrial world. But over recent years they have become a major subject of controversy for many consumers. On the one hand it is claimed that our food in the West has never been more safe, attractive, nutritious and plentiful. More than ever before consumers are free from the dangers of food poisoning from spoiled foods or food-borne organisms thanks to modern refrigeration, advanced canning and food-processing techniques such as freeze-drying, ultra-high-temperature treatment and aseptic packaging, and by the use of pre-servatives and other chemical additives. Preservatives in food are not new. Fruit has been preserved in sugar since the Middle Ages and 2000 years ago salt and smoke were used to preserve meat and fish in China – although according to modern theories, smoked foods may be a health hazard. In the modern food industry chemicals replace colour and flavour that may have been lost in processing and storage; others inhibit the separation of oils in mayonnaises and keep bacteria and moulds from spoiling foods. But it is claimed by some that the same modern chemical additives that provide protection from food poisoning can in themselves be a danger to health.

Our heightened awareness of what we eat has led us to question the origins and background of our food. Progress in agricultural science and pressures on producers to supply more food more economically have led to the increasing use of chemical fertilisers and pesticides. Now there is growing concern that minute quantities of these chemicals may build up inside our bodies and gradually poison us.

Other dangers also appear in food as a direct result of the advances made in agricultural and food technology. In Britain the cattle disease bovine spongiform encephalopathy (BSE) is said to have originated as a result of including sheep's heads, which could have been infected with scrapie (a disease similar to BSE), in the manufacture of high-protein cattle feed, aimed at improving milk yield. It has resulted in considerable public unease and sharply reduced beef consumption. There has been a similar outcry, also in Britain, against the genetic engineering of our food, which has all sorts of implications for our nutrition in the future. The implantation of hormones in cows to improve their milk production has already been tested but is not allowed in Britain and the use of growth-promoting hormones, such as anabolic agents in beef cattle, has been banned throughout the EC.

However, some of our food worries result not from the effects of technological developments but from a lack of technology. For many years salmonella has been endemic in many poultry flocks throughout the world. It is sometimes popularly thought that its spread has been encouraged by factory farming and this has caused new outcries because technology cannot cure it.

A healthy diet

Probably never in the history of food have there been so many consumers so aware of what they are eating, so conscious of what they should eat, and with so much information to guide them. Nowadays diet and health are seen as closely connected. Most people no longer regard food in terms of staving off hunger or for the pleasure of good food alone but rather as an aid to improving their quality of life. A healthy diet can be the pathway to an active and long life. From chemist William Prout's first division of foods into saccharina (carbohydrates), oleosia (fats) and albuminosa (proteins) in 1825, nutritional science has grown into its modern, highly developed and vocal state. Diets of every conceivable kind are offered to the reading public: low-fat, high-fibre, high-protein, low-carbohydrate, slimmer's diets, heart diets, low-cholesterol inducing diets, gluten-free, macrobiotic, and vegetarian.

Diets in themselves are not new. In India the Jains were strict vegetarians before the time of Christ. Vegetarian diets have appeared throughout history – Saint Augustine in the fifth century ate no meat. By the sixth century AD the rule of St Benedict – the basic code for European monastic life – laid down that throughout the year monks were forbidden the flesh of quadrupeds except when they were sick; on the year's 200 fast days they were only allowed one vegetarian meal a day. Buddhist cooks in China during the fifteenth century developed amazing skills in creating dishes which looked and tasted like meat, even down to the bones, but were in fact vegetarian. People followed vegetarian diets for a variety of reasons. Some, like the Jains and Chinese Buddhists, believed that it was wrong to take any life even for food. Others, like the early Christians, believed that abstinence for the body was good for the soul, and yet others thought that man was healthier without animal flesh. In the fifteenth century an Italian doctor recommended his ageing patient not to eat goose, duck, lamb and pork, especially if it were fresh. He was also to avoid meat pies and 'every other dish which coarsens and clogs the blood'. At the beginning of the eighteenth century as a boy of sixteen, Benjamin Franklin tried following a vegetarian diet, having been influenced by Thomas Tryon's arguments against the taking of any life in *The Way to Health, Long Life and Happiness*, but abandoned it a few years later on the reflection that since fish ate other fish they could themselves be eaten. Dr John Harvey Kellogg, the originator of Kelloggs cornflakes, was a strong believer in a vegetarian diet and wrote, 'There is nothing necessary or desirable for human nutrition to be found in meats or flesh foods which is not found in and derived from vegetable products'.

Other people have followed special diets or eaten particular dishes to improve their health or appearance. Byron is reported to have gone on a diet

MANNERS AND MODES.

DYSPEPSIA DE LUXE.

A wry look at dieting in a cartoon from Punch *in the 1920s.*

of boiled potatoes and vinegar to reduce his weight. However, what is new in the modern age is the weight of nutritional information and publicity which accompany the diets of today. Diets for slimmers of every conceivable kind appear in numerous books and magazines. They have included a Swedish diet limited to the water in which unpeeled potatoes have been boiled or, in complete contrast, a French diet of steak and red wine. Alongside diets, people have bought quack medicines since the earliest times to improve their looks, health or reduce their weight and have been criticised for their vanity as in the fifteenth-century sermon, 'Yet schalt thou dye for all that physik'.

The search for the exotic

Today our affluent well-fed society in the West is able to choose what it will eat and our newfound awareness of the quality of our foods has changed our shopping habits. Even in small supermarkets foods from around the world are on the shelves. Increasingly in Europe and North America it is also possible to buy vegetables and fruit grown organically in conditions free from chemical pesticides and fertilisers. Modern medical recommendations for a healthy diet include reducing the daily fat intake, particularly of animal fat, and including more fibre in our diets – so margarines high in polyunsaturates, low-fat yoghurts and skimmed milk are increasingly popular, while brown bread now has a higher status than white bread which was for so long the benchmark of good living.

We also adopt foods from other cultures. Beancurd or tofu, for 1000 years a cheap and valuable source of vegetable protein in the East, is now sold widely in Western supermarkets. Bulgar or bulgur wheat, a staple grain food from the Middle East whose origins go back 3000 years, now features in modern Western recipes. Yoghurt is also an accepted item in Western European cooking. People are seeking foods they consider to be healthy as well as good to eat, and modern cookery books reflect this trend as in this recipe from Anne Lindsay's *Smart Cooking: quick and tasty recipes for healthy living.*

BULGAR WHEAT, TOFU AND SWEET PEPPERS

This main-course vegetarian dish is a good source of protein and fiber. If possible use bulgar instead of cracked wheat, it has a nuttier, richer flavor and takes less time to cook.

1 cup (250 ml) coarse or medium bulgar or cracked wheat
2 tbsp (25 ml) butter
3 cloves garlic, minced
2 tsp (10 ml) ground cumin
2 sweet red peppers, seeded and cut into strips
3 tbsp (45 ml) vinegar
$\frac{1}{3}$ cup (75 ml) water
1 packet (10 oz/284 g) fresh spinach, washed, stemmed and cut into strips
1 tsp (5 ml) salt
freshly ground pepper
$\frac{3}{4}$ lb (350 g) firm style tofu or beancurd, cut into cubes

Rinse bulgar under cold water. Place in bowl and add enough cold water to cover by 2 inches/5 cm; soak for 1 hour. Drain thoroughly in sieve.

In large skillet, melt butter over medium heat, add garlic and cook for a few seconds. Stir in cumin, then peppers. Cover and cook for 5 minutes.

Add bulgar, vinegar, and water; cook, uncovered, for 5 minutes or until bulgar is nearly tender; stirring often (cracked wheat will take about 15 minutes longer; add more water as necessary). Add spinach, stir until mixed and spinach is slightly wilted. Season with salt and pepper to taste. Add tofu; cover and simmer for 5 minutes or until heated through and flavours are blended. Makes 6 main-course servings.

Calories per serving: 252
Grams fat per serving: 7
Fiber: Excellent
Vitamins A and C and iron: Excellent
Niacin and phosphorus: Good

Alongside the desire for healthy eating there is also a move towards the frankly exotic in food. It is a style which searches out the new and borrows and combines ingredients and flavours from around the world. It can be found in different forms everywhere in the prosperous industrial countries of the world. Chinese cuisine in Hong Kong, while remaining Chinese, has adapted and widened to include new food flavours. In Japan mild curry sauces make popular dishes at family meals, while McDonalds do a roaring trade in the centre of Tokyo. In Western Europe today south-east Asian sauces and styles of cooking occupy the pages of fashionable magazines. The search for the new and upbeat is motivated partly by the images collected on holidays spent in faraway places, and partly by a feeling that the familiar has been with us for a long time and it is time for a change. In Britain, with the abandonment of much everyday cooking in favour of convenience foods, when people do cook they are more adventurous and seek out more demanding recipes and more unusual ingredients. It is not by chance that venison is farmed in many parts of the country. Experiments in the farming of wild boar – a contradiction in terms – are in process and farmed salmon and trout are commonplace on every fish-stall. Some people are willing to travel quite long distances to find particular foods for special occasions. New businesses involving small producers making cheeses from goats' and sheeps' milk, and smoke houses experimenting with smoked meats and poultry as well as fish are appearing throughout the country. Regionalism is developing afresh. Cooking has probably never been so exciting; caution has been thrown to the winds – we are ready to try anything so long as it is new. An example of this kind of cooking is to be found in the BBC's *Good Food* magazine. In the recipe below none of the salad ingredients could have been bought in Britain twenty-five years ago, and smoked chicken, mangoes and oak leaf lettuce have only appeared in the last ten years.

SMOKED CHICKEN SALAD WITH MINT AND HONEY DRESSING

SERVES 4

---

2 smoked chicken breasts, finely sliced

---

1 fresh mango, peeled and sliced

---

oak leaf lettuce leaves

---

1 avocado, sliced at the last minute

For the dressing

---

2 tbsp finely chopped fresh mint

---

1 tbsp clear honey

---

2 tbsp vegetable oil

---

3 tbsp cider vinegar

---

seasoning

---

1 Make the dressing: place all the ingredients in a screw-topped jar and shake well.

2 Prepare the mango, lettuce and avocado. Arrange the chicken together with the salad ingredients on a large plate and spoon over the dressing. Serve straight away.

In the same issue of the *Good Food* magazine nearly 50 per cent of the recipes contained novel ingredients of one kind or another which could not have been found in British supermarkets twenty years ago. As we have seen, food through the centuries has been influenced by fashion and people's taste for the new, but in the twentieth century the speed of change has accelerated. The *nouvelle cuisine* of the eighties is a thing of the past; today chefs and food writers alike struggle to anticipate the next fashion.

BIBLIOGRAPHY

ABUL FAZL ALLAMI *Ain I Akbari* trans. by
H. Blockmann, Calcutta: 1873.

ACTON, ELIZA *Modern Cookery* London:
Longmans, 1845.

Adam's luxury and Eve's Cookery London:
Dodsley & Cooper, 1744.

ALLCHIN, BRIDGET AND RAYMOND
The Birth of Indian Civilization
Harmondsworth: Penguin, 1968.

ALTSCHUL, AARON M., ed. *New Protein
Foods: Vol. 2 – Technology Part B*
New York: Academic Press, 1976.

ANDERSON, E. N. *The Food of China*
New Haven: Yale University Press, 1988.

APICIUS *The Roman Cookery Book*
trans. Barbara Flower and Elisabeth
Rosenbaum, London: Harrap, 1958.

ATHENAEUS *The Deipnosophists* trans. C. B.
Gulick, London: Heinemann, 1927.

AUSTIN, THOMAS
Two Fifteenth Century Cookery Books
Early English Text Society, 1888.

BALSDON, J. P. V. D. *Life and Leisure in Ancient
Rome* London: Bodley Head, 1969.

BARBIER, EDMUND JEAN-FRANÇOIS
*Journal d'un bourgeois de Paris sous le règne
de Louis XV*
Paris: Union Générale d'Editions, 1963.

BEAUNE, COLETTE, ed. *Journal d'un bourgeois de
Paris à la fin de la guerre de Cent Ans*
Paris: Livre de Poche, 1990.

BEETON, ISABELLA *The Book of Household
Management* London: Beeton, 1861.

Dictionary of Everyday Cookery
London: Beeton, 1864.

BOORDE, ANDREW *A Compendyous Regyment or
a Dyetary of Helth* Wyer, 1542.

BRAUDEL, FERNAND *Capitalism and Material
Life 1400–1800* London: Fontana, 1974.

BRERETON, GEORGINE AND FERRIER, JANET
Ménagier de Paris Oxford: Clarendon, 1981.

BRIGGS, RICHARD *The Art of Cookery*
London: 1788.

BROCK, ARTHUR JOHN *Greek Medicine*
London: Dent, 1929.

BURNETT, JOHN *Plenty and Want: a Social
History of Diet in England from 1815 to
the Present Day* London: Nelson, 1966.

CADILLAC AND LIETTE
The Western Country in the Seventeenth Century
Chicago: Lakeside Press, 1947.

CARCOPINO, JEROME *Daily Life in Ancient
Rome* London: Routledge, 1941.

CARÊME, MARIE ANTONIN *L'art de la cuisine
française au dix-neuvième siècle* 5 vols.,
Paris: 1833–47.

CHAFIN, MARY *Original Country Recipes*
London: Macmillan, 1979.

CHAKRAVARTY, INDIRA *Saga of Indian Food*
New Delhi: Sterling, 1972.

CHRISTENSEN, ARTHUR *L'Iran sous les Sassanides* Copenhagen: Ejnar Munksgaard, 1944.

CROOKE, WILLIAM, ed. *Fryer's East India and Persia* vol. 3 (Series II), Cambridge: Hakluyt Society, 1915.

DALGAIRNS, MRS *The Practice of cookery* Edinburgh: Cadell, 1829.

DAVIES, ROY W. *Service in the Roman army* Edinburgh: Edinburgh University Press, 1989.

DIGBY, SIR KENELM, BART. *The Queen's Closet Opened* London: 1665.

DION, ROGER *Histoire de la vigne et du vin en France* Paris: Flammarion, 1977.

DRUMMOND, JACK CECIL AND WILBRAHAM, ANNE *The Englishman's Food* London: Cape, 1939.

DUDLEY, DONALD *Roman Society* Harmondsworth: Penguin, 1978.

DUVERNOY, JEAN 'La nourriture en Languedoc à l'époque Cathare' in *Carcassonne et sa région: Actes de XL et XXIV* (Congrès d'études), Carcassonne: Centre national de recherche scientifique, 1970.

EDEN, FREDERICK MORTON *The State of the Poor* 3 vols., London: 1797.

ENGELS, FRIEDRICH *The Condition of the Working Class in England* Leipzig: 1845.

FARMER, FANNY *Boston Cookery School Cookbook* Boston: Little, Brown, 1909.

FENTON, ALEXANDER AND KISBAN, ESZTER, eds. *Food in Change – Eating Habits from the Middle Ages to the Present Day* Edinburgh: John Donald, 1986.

FETTIPLACE, ELINOR *Elinor Fettiplace's Receipt Book* ed. H. Spurling, Harmondsworth: Penguin, 1987.

FIELDHOUSE, PAUL *Food and Nutrition: Customs and Culture* London: Croom Helm, 1985.

FRANCATELLI, CHARLES *The Cook's Guide and Housekeeper's and Butler's Assistant* London: 1862.

GERARD, JOHN *The Herball and generall histories of plantes* London: 1597.

GLASSE, HANNAH *The Art of Cookery made plain and easy* London: 1747.

GOGLIN, JEAN-LOUIS *Les misérables dans l'Occident médiéval* Paris: Editions du Seuil, 1976.

GOLTEIN, S.D. *A Mediterranean Society* vols. 1 and 4 Berkeley: University of California Press, 1967, 1983.

Letters of Medieval Jewish Traders Princetown: Princetown University Press, 1973.

DE GONCOURT, EDMOND AND JULES *Journal* 3 vols., Paris: Robert Laffont, 1989.

GRIGSON, JANE *Fish Cookery* Harmondsworth: Penguin, 1975.

GUTHRIE, DOUGLAS *A History of Medicine* London: Nelson, 1945.

HENISCH, BRIDGET ANN *Fast and Feast* London: Pennsylvania State University Press, 1976.

HIBBERT, CHRISTOPHER *The destruction of Lord Raglan* London: Longmans, 1961.

HOBHOUSE, HENRY *Seeds of Change* London: Sidgwick & Jackson, 1985.

JAFFREY, MADHUR *Eastern Vegetarian Cooking* London: Cape, 1983.

KOSAMBI, DAMODAR *The Culture and Civilisation of Ancient India* London: Routledge & Kegan Paul, 1965.

An Introduction to the Study of Indian History Bombay: Popular Prakashan, 1975.

LANGLAND, WILLIAM *The Vision of Piers Plowman* trans. T. Tiller, London: BBC, 1981.

LA VARENNE, FRANÇOIS *Le Cuisinier François* Paris: 1686.

LECLANT, JEAN 'Coffee and Cafés in Paris, 1644–1693' in FORSTER, R. and RANUM, O. eds. *Food and Drink in History, selections from 'Annales'* vol. 5, Baltimore: Johns Hopkins University Press, 1979.

LEEMING, MARGARET AND HUANG, MAY *Dimsum* London: Macdonald, 1985.

Far-Eastern Vegetarian Cooking London: Columbus, 1985.

The Chinese Food Tradition London: Duckworth, forthcoming.

LEEMING, MARGARET AND KOHSAKA, M. *Japanese Cookery* London: Rider, 1984.

'Liji (Record of Ritual)' in MULLER, F. Max *Sacred Books of the East* trans. J. Legge, Oxford: Clarendon, 1885.

LINDSAY, ANNE *Smart Cooking: quick and tasty recipes for healthy living* Toronto: Macmillan of Canada, 1986.

LOAHARANU, PAISAN 'International Developments in Food Irradiation' in GHEE, Ang How, ed., *Trends in Food Product Development* Singapore: World Congress of Food Science & Technology, 1987.

MARKHAM, GERVASE *The English Hus-wife* London: 1615.

MASSIALOT, FRANÇOIS *Le Cuisinier roial et bourgeois* Paris: 1691.

MAY, ROBERT *The Accomplish't Cook* London: 1660.

MCGEE, HAROLD *On Food and Cooking* London: Allen & Unwin, 1986.

MILLER, J. INNES *The Spice Trade of the Roman Empire* Oxford: Clarendon, 1969.

MINNS, RAYNES *Bombers and Mash – the Domestic Front 1939–45* London: Virago, 1980.

MITCHELL, R. J. AND LEYS, M. D. R. *History of London Life* Harmondsworth: Penguin, 1963.

MOLIÈRE *The Citizen Turned Gentleman* trans. Baker & Miller, London: 1739.

MONTEUX, H. *Conservation de santé et prolongation de vie* Paris; 1572.

NELSON, WILLIAM, ed. *A Fifteenth Century School Book* Oxford: Clarendon, 1956.

ORIGO, IRIS *The Merchant of Prato* Harmondsworth: Penguin, 1963.

PEPYS, SAMUEL *Diary of Samuel Pepys* ed. R. Latham and W. Matthews 11 vols., London: Bell, 1970–76.

PLINY *Natural History* various edns.

PRICE, REBECCA *The Compleat Cook* London: Routledge & Kegan Paul, 1974.

RODEN, CLAUDIA *A Book of Middle Eastern Food* Harmondsworth: Penguin, 1970.

'Early Arab Cooking and Cookery Manuscripts' in *Petits Propos Culinaires* 6, 1980.

ROUCHE, MICHEL 'La faim à l'époque Carolingienne' in *Revue Historique* 1973 pp. 295–320.

ROWNTREE, SEEBOHM *Poverty: A Study of Town Life* London: Nelson, 1901.

SCHIAFFINO, MARIAROSA *Chocolate* Exeter: Webb & Bower, 1989.

'Shi Jin' (Book of Odes) in *The Chinese Classics* vol. 4, trans. J. Legge, London, 1871.

SHINODA, OSAMIS *Chugoku shokubutsu shi* (History of Food in China) Tokyo: 1974.

SIMMONS, AMELIA *American Cookery* Hartford, Connecticut, 1796.

SINCLAIR, JOHN *The Statistical Account of Scotland* vol. IV, Edinburgh: 1795.

SOYER, ALEXIS *The Modern Housewife* London: Simpkin, Marshall & Co., 1849.

STEEDMAN, CAROLINE *The Radical Soldier's Tale* London: Routledge & Kegan Paul, 1988.

TAILLEVENT *Le viandier de Guillaume Tirel dit Taillevent* ed. Baron Jerome Pichon, Paris: Techener, 1892.

TALBOT, C. H. *Medicine in Medieval England* London: Oldbourne, 1967.

TANNAHILL, REAY *Food in History* Harmondsworth: Penguin, new edn. 1988.

THOMPSON, FLORA *Lark Rise to Candleford* Harmondsworth: Penguin, 1973.

The Travels of Ibn Battuta vol. 3 ed. Gibb, Cambridge: Hakluyt Society, 1971.

The Travels of Leo Rozmital ed. M. Letts, Cambridge: Hakluyt Society, 1957.

VICKERY, KENTON FRANK *Food in Early Greece* Chicago: Ares Inc., 1980.

WARNER, RICHARD, ed. *Antiquitates culinariae* 1791.

WILLAN, ANN *Great Cooks and their Recipes* London: Elm Tree, 1977.

WILSON, C. ANNE *Food and Drink in Britain* Harmondsworth: Penguin, 1976.

'The Saracen Connection: Arab Cuisine and the Medieval West' in *Petits Propos Culinaires* 7 & 8, 1981.

WOODFORDE, JAMES *The Diary of a Country Parson* ed. J. Beresford 5 vols. Humphrey Milford, 1924.

The Ansford Diary of James Woodforde ed. R. L. Winstanley 2 vols. Parson Woodforde Society, 1979–80.

WRIGHT, J. E. AND CORBETT, DORIS *Pioneer Life* Pittsburgh: University of Pittsburgh Press, 1940.

INDEX

Page numbers in *italics* refer to pages with illustrations.

PICTURE CREDITS

Page 2 Michael Holford; 3 & 5 Mansell Collection; 10 Colchester Archaeological Trust; 13 & 14 from *Wen Wu* 10, 1981; 16 Ann Ronan Picture Library; 18 from *The Culture & Civilization of Ancient India* by D. D. Kosambi, Routledge & Kegan Paul, 1965; 20 Ann & Bury Peerless; 24 from *Zhongguo pengren shi lue* by Tao Wentai, Nanjing 1983; 30 Victoria & Albert Museum; 33 Werner Forman Archive; 35 from *Zhongguo pengren shi lue* by Tao Wentai, Nanjing 1983; 40 from *Yin shan zheng yao* by Hu Sihui, Beijing 1985; 46 Ann & Bury Peerless; 49 British Library; 51 & 55 Hulton Picture Company; 59 from *One Hundred Manuscripts in the Collection of Henry Yates Thompson Vol. VI*, Chiswick Press, 1916; 60 H. Roger-Viollet; 63 British Library; 67 Mansell Collection; 72 *both* Hulton Picture Company; 75 Mary Evans Picture Library; 76 Bibliothèque Nationale, Paris; 79 Mary Evans Picture Library; 80 & 86 Hulton Picture Company; 87 Mary Evans Picture Library; 91 Johnny van Haeften Gallery, London/Bridgeman Art Library; 95 *both* Hulton Picture Company; 97 Giraudon; 100 & 102 Hulton Picture Company; 105 from *Food & Drink, a Pictorial Archive from Nineteenth-Century Sources*, Dover Publications Inc., 1980; 107 Royal Botanic Gardens, Kew; 111 & 113 Mary Evans Picture Library; 114 Victoria & Albert Museum/ Bridgeman Art Library; 123 & 124 Mary Evans Picture Library; 127 Hulton Picture Company; 128 Mary Evans Picture Library; 130 Hulton Picture Company; 133 Royal Commission on Historical Monuments (England); 135 Bridgeman Art Library; 136 Mary Evans Picture Library; 140 Hulton Picture Company; 142 & 145 Mary Evans Picture Library; 148 Hulton Picture Company; 150 Birmingham City Art Gallery & Museum; 151 Hulton Picture Company; 152 from *Mrs Beeton's Book of Household Management* 1861; 156 E. T. Archive; 159 & 162 Hulton Picture Company; 163 Imperial War Museum; 167 Central Office of Information; 168 J. Sainsbury plc; 172 Mary Evans Picture Library.

TEXT CREDITS

We are grateful to the following for permission to reproduce copyright material:
Harrap Publishing Group Ltd for extracts from *The Roman Cookery Book* by B. Flower and E. Rosenbaum, 1978; Jonathan Cape and Rogers, Coleridge & White Ltd for 'Geeli Khichri' from *Eastern Vegetarian Cooking* by Madhur Jaffrey, 1983; David Higham Associates for 'Cold Chicken Sofrito' from *A Book of Middle Eastern Food* by Claudia Roden, published by Penguin Books Ltd; The Hakluyt Society for extracts from *The travels of Ibn Battuta, 1325–1354, Vol. III*, translated and edited by Professor Sir Hamilton Gibb, 1971; The Hakluyt Society for extracts from *A new account of East India and Persia, 1672–1681* by John Fryer, Vol. III, edited by William Crooke, 1915; The Hakluyt Society for extracts from *The travels of Leo Rozmital, 1465–1467*, translated and edited by Malcolm Letts, 1957; Penguin Books Ltd in association with Jonathan Cape (1963) for an extract from *The Merchant of Prato* by Iris Origo copyright 1957, 1963; Routledge for extracts from *The Compleat Cook* by Rebecca Price, edited by M. Masson, 1974; Routledge for extracts from *The Radical Soldier's Tale* by Caroline Steedman, 1988; Birmingham City Museum and Art Gallery for an extract from *A Taste of Change*, 1985; David Higham Associates for extracts from *The Destruction of Lord Raglan* by Christopher Hibbert, published by Penguin Books Ltd; The Best of Bridge Publishing Ltd for 'Seafood Scallop Shells' from *Royal Treats for Entertaining*; Macmillan of Canada, a Division of Canada Publishing Corporation for 'Bulgar Wheat, Tofu and Sweet Peppers' from *Smart Cooking* by Anne Lindsay, 1986; Hudson and Halls for 'Smoked Chicken Salad with Mint and Honey Dressing'.